Proxemics and the Architecture
of Social Interaction

Larry D. Busbea

Columbia Books on Architecture and the City

There is, of course, the architecture we inhabit, that we design and use as object, image, and carapace. There are also the intangible architectures we carry with us—bodily limits, affordances, our range of possibilities, frames of reference. Then there are those psychical and perceptual architectures that inhabit us and flow through us—drives, structures, filters, distributions; patterns inherent or instilled. But what are the consequences of allowing architecture to slip from the physical to the figurative in this way? Haven't we simply moved from the literal to the metaphorical? And mightn't such a slippage constitute a strategic or even cynical attempt to expand the purview of design to that of life itself? Perhaps. But such an expansion or slippage isn't unprecedented. And it wasn't always cynical.

This book is a document of a historical moment when the social sciences and design disciplines began to recognize these architectures as accessible and observable; when myriad fields attempted to visualize the overlapping movements of the existential, political, and technical structures from which subjectivity itself was extruded. Further, these developments were inextricable from an emerging ethos of design that conflated the prognostic capacities of the social sciences with emerging categories of experience that could only be described in the language of aesthetics. Exhaustively tracing the contours of these historical, disciplinary, and perceptual developments would require a vantage that was impossibly distant from them, a contrived object language retrofitted for the description of pure pattern. Sixty years ago, the limits of such descriptive systems—linguistic, algorithmic, diagrammatic, mimetic—were apparent to researchers faced with the complexity of what would come to be called *environment*. New ones seemed necessary.

Proxemics was one such system. Ubiquitous in the 1960s and 70s, proxemics appeared as social scientists were newly describing humanity as a powerful environmental agent, but an agent acutely subjected to the conditioning mechanisms of that environment. Proxemics was developed to describe the patterns of this very paradox—to quantify the ways in which our contingent perception of reality is imperfectly projected onto a world almost entirely of our own creation. "*Man and his environment participate in molding each other*," anthropologist Edward T. Hall, the inventor of proxemics, wrote. "Man is now in the position of actually creating the total world in which he lives, what the ethologists refer to as his biotope. In creating this world he is actually determining *what kind of organism* he will be."[1]

More concretely, proxemics was a notation system for recording human interactions with others and their surroundings. Pictographic and numerical, the system was able, according to Hall, to capture body position, biological efferents, and communicational comportments that subjects themselves were unaware of. Hall devised technical equipment to scrutinize these data and aggregated them into sets to reveal previously invisible psychological, cultural, and ethnic patterns of interaction. He concluded that subjects carry these patterns with them as virtual frames or "bubbles" around which they unconsciously organize their milieus, and through which certain behaviors and perceptions are facilitated (and precluded). Hall eventually would conclude that these proxemic bubbles were divisive cultural apparatuses that had to be recognized as such in order to be transcended.[2]

Like proxemics itself, this book is dedicated to grasping the vicissitudes of these interactions—not as conventional objects, or (merely) as a historically conditioned set of social, political, or technical mechanisms, but as a category or modality of perception. This category diverges epistemologically and aesthetically from conventional models of identifying objects and subjects of research in that it does not necessarily isolate a figure on a ground or an object in a space but instead recognizes a human environment replete with material and immaterial forces, forms, events, and constructions simultaneously internal and external to the subject.

That Hall fashioned the science of proxemics as an anthropological method should not dissuade those of us in other disciplines from attending to its aspirations, its precise applications, or its failures. On the contrary, these attributes divulge its hybrid and prodigal status: not existing solely as a data aggregation device, but rather as a comprehensive visualization technique for structures both spatial and temporal, real and imagined. For proxemics was empirically grounded in the geopolitical chaos of the 1960s and 70s as much as it was a metaphysical repository for aesthetic and epistemological propositions. It was both a grand unified theory of existence and an *application* to be deployed in the most circumscribed situations. Its resolution was also perpetually deferred, always being elaborated and modified to accommodate unforeseen variables. It seemed to be burrowing into the very fabric of reality even as it scattered to the furthest peripheries of perception. It presumed to trace environmental patterns already in place, just as it promised a means to produce new patterns. Ostensibly a tool for describing conditions, proxemics forever folded in on itself in continuous self-critique.

But these paradoxical dyads can no more describe proxemics than proxemics could reliably describe reality. This was not merely a method applied by an observer to a specific phenomenon (object, subject, or interaction) in a given context. It was *context* itself expanded and materialized—context absorbing the previously distinct categories of object, method, and observing apparatus. In this sense, proxemics was central to a postwar revival of earlier models of *milieu* and *Umwelt*, only now subjected to a new regime of verifiability.[3] To put this in simple terms that will nonetheless confound the normative epistemological assumptions of art history: proxemics was an attempt to describe *context as form*.

Perhaps one last dyadic abstraction might help justify documenting proxemics as a historical and aesthetic artifact of significance. Proxemics could have taken the form of an endlessly elaborated philosophy of human situatedness, of everyday life, of ideology critique; it might have been a theory of alienation, or a periodization (similar to postindustrialism). To a certain extent it aspired to all of these functions, but it did so as a hyper-pragmatic approach to the observation and recording of humans interacting with one another and the world around them. It sought to systematically score the postures and activities of life, input those scored phenomena into a real database, and extract the data when needed, not only for social interpretation but also for application to governmental policy and design decisions. It did this via technical apparatuses of observation, syncretic and iterative modes of notation, and overtures to a design community who, it was hoped, might implement its outcomes. And while its inventor made every attempt to efface the mediating structures that might have corrupted its objectivity, the most tangible remains of this method are the material traces of those structures: photographs, charts, diagrams, and the very technical devices used to assure its transparency.

Which brings us to the purpose of the present volume, which is a counterintuitive project, to be sure. It takes as its object not an object but a method, which, in turn, was a dispersed and emergent set of intuitions about environmental determinism and relativism. Instead of inquiring into the content of said method—its outcomes—this book examines its structures, its physical residues, and its assimilation into other disciplines (namely, architecture). To phrase this again in terms familiar to art history: this project does not explicate the content of proxemics so much as attend to its forms. Indeed, if there is a thesis contained among this text and attendant archival fragments, it is that proxemics was a visual apparatus developed at a time when human subjectivity was both extended and thrown into question by new conceptions of environmental agency and coercive determination. It was a system for literally tracing the patterns of these complimentary forces, for trying to *see* them for the first time.

Hall's most famous book, *The Hidden Dimension* (1966), appeared as the notion of social constructionism was coalescing across the human sciences. Peter Berger and Thomas Luckmann's *The Social Construction of Reality* was published the same year. This was also when Marshall McLuhan was articulating the idea of human "extensions" as both facilitative and interpellative devices (the term "extension" actually came from Hall) and Thomas Kuhn was reframing the assumptions of scientific empiricism with the notion of "paradigms."[4] In Europe, philosophers were contending with similar questions of linguistic, institutional, and biopolitical subject formation.[5] In a more pragmatic register, Hall understood "culture" as a system of coercive rules that influenced the subject's understanding of reality and their capacity for action within it but that remained, as Hall frequently put it, "out-of-awareness." His view was analogous to Berger and Luckmann's concern with what they described evocatively as "the plasticity of the human organism and its susceptibility to socially determined interference."[6] Proxemics functioned in Hall's project, therefore, not as a simple descriptive tool but as a device for measuring this plasticity, and for bringing the processes of what is often called social construction—though he seldom used this phrase—into view.

But these processes are all the more obscure or unconscious precisely because of the constructed nature of *perception* itself. Daily life could hardly proceed if we were constantly aware of the ways in which our language, institutions, and environments are actively constraining and shaping us. For Hall, it was as if the effectiveness of culture were premised on its self-effacement. In this sense, the forms with which proxemics was concerned were not only objects of perception but also *aspects* of perception, and something of the circularity of these observations inflected Hall's work. His was a paranoiac project, infused always with a sense that *he* could see a world that others could not, and that their language and paradigms prevented them from grasping its mechanisms. His only recourse was the comparative study of patterns, to observe the behaviors of members of one culture and superimpose them onto another—like to observe that Americans deal with personal space differently than Arabs, that Mexicans understand money in fundamentally different ways than the Japanese, or that children communicate in a "high context" format while scientists rely on a "low context" symbolic language, and so on.[7] It was a project fixed uncomfortably between existential speculation and the basest types of essentialism.

Nonetheless, Hall hoped he could visualize, map, and model the lines of interference that emerged from these overlapping spatiotemporal patterns, and make others aware of them. Proxemics tantalizingly promised a concrete method for effecting a kind of gestalt reversal of figure and ground that would allow environment itself to advance as an object of perception, observation, and, as we shall see, design. This essay and the archival documents that follow trace this movement: the historical emergence of proxemics as perceptual apparatus and subsequent attempts to operationalize its outcomes through architectural and design initiatives that sought to reconceptualize the human-environment interface. Unlike the extant literature on Hall and his method, this book does not attempt to ascertain the fitness of proxemics as a prognostic or diagnostic tool for the social sciences.[8] Rather, it treats it as a historical phenomenon with its own intellectual sources and material traces, many of which were absorbed into the discipline of architecture.

The book comprises two parts: this introductory text and a selection of images from Hall's archive.[9] Some of these images were published, but most were not. They function (for Hall, and us) metonymically: surreptitious photographs of groups of people slide over those of animals in their habitats (natural or otherwise), map onto comic strips and newspaper clippings, expand out again via pictures of offices and public spaces—famous and quotidian buildings and environments—and translate into more formal iterations as drawings, notations, and charts that break down and categorize proxemic complexities. No single image here, nor their comprehensive sum, will provide a key to the vagaries of Hall's project. They attest instead to proxemics' perpetual deferral, and its creator's attempt to visualize the ether of existential and political life. These materials were Hall's tools, evidence, method, and proof for his theories regarding the very substance of spatial interaction.

Might it be possible to grasp this substance? Might such substance be used to cast new types of human environments that would ameliorate the alienation and reification of contemporary life? Could new architectures be conceived that would actually facilitate human activities instead of circumscribe them? That might accommodate human diversity, reconnect people, and reconcile the harsh paradoxes of urban existence? Could the emerging field of environmental design become a scientifically grounded form of psycho-social ergonomics? From its inception, proxemics was both a research method and an operative set of propositions about the built environment. As it evolved, Hall never stopped his active dialogs with designers, learning from architects even as he offered them his expertise through consulting and lecturing. This book is about these feedback loops, and it is therefore a historicization of not just proxemics but the ways in which the design disciplines attempted to assimilate and instrumentalize human data in the broadest sense.

BACKGROUND(S)

Edward T. Hall spent the summer of 1949—his first as an assistant professor at Bennington College—in his basement painstakingly constructing fifteen geodesic domes out of copper wire.[10] This compulsive project took shape after R. Buckminster Fuller's daughter Allegra (a Bennington student) introduced Fuller to Hall and his wife Mildred Reed Hall following their move to Bennington the previous fall. Hall had become obsessive about deciphering his new friend's nonlinear, expansive geometric thinking through his distinctive patterns. Indeed, Fuller's great circles—or bubbles, perhaps—were merely one manifestation of Hall's engagement with formalized pattern. He had begun his academic career training in archaeology, fascinated by the geometries of Hopi pottery sherds. This was followed by a span at the University of Arizona's dendrochronology laboratory, where he studied the concentric circles of tree rings, searching for tiny variations in their density and thickness—indices of climatological events in the distant past.[11] Hall's intuitive attraction to these manmade and natural geometries must have been validated by his mentor Ruth Benedict's seminal theorization of the "patterns of culture," which she was no doubt still elaborating while Hall worked with her during his graduate studies at Columbia University in the early 1940s.[12]

Hall's intellectual formation took place at the end of certain disciplinary trajectories in anthropology and at the beginning of radical new ones. The anecdotal, cross-cultural sampling of his popular publications is clearly of a piece with the tradition of "culture-and-personality" studies initiated earlier in the twentieth century by one of Hall's heroes, the anthropologist Franz Boas, as much as with the "national character" studies that emerged in the 1940s. In accordance with these developments, Hall's work can be placed—alongside Benedict and Claude Lévi-Strauss—within a historical tendency to shift the locus of anthropological research from an exoticized other to the domestic environment.[13] Indeed, Hall participated alongside friend Margaret Mead and others in Benedict's Columbia seminar on culture and personality. As Fred Turner has recently argued, these developments within the discipline offered a way to anthropologically verify (and cultivate) certain psychological characteristics that would enhance subjective (American) agency in the modern world and might re-center the subject in a rich and empowering communicational milieu.[14] While Hall was sympathetic to the progressive ideals of Benedict and Mead, for instance, his own work would focus on the conditioning mechanisms of culture more than any stable character attributes resulting from those mechanisms.[15] In addition to these contemporaneous trends, Hall's work, which so often questioned the assumptions and limits of his own activities, also foreshadowed the reflexive turn that would characterize an emerging critical anthropological theory in the 1980s.

Paradoxically, since he was clearly interested in the malleability of culture, Hall made a much stronger appeal to biology than many of his contemporaries. The field of ethology in particular would lend itself to his methods of describing the interactional nature of human behavior, always co-forming with its surroundings. A series of meetings with the Swiss ethologist and Zurich zoo director Heini Hediger would prove foundational to Hall's articulation of proxemics. The insights gleaned from Hediger's theories on the micro-climates of zoo enclosures would soon coalesce with J. B. Calhoun's famous studies of the behavior of rats in overcrowded conditions and other biological work that demonstrated certain psychosomatic phenomena that could all too easily be projected onto seemingly comparable human conditions, such as urban crowding.

This strange admixture of biological determinism and cultural relativism would complicate the reception of Hall's work throughout his career. He largely failed to find validation within his own scientific discipline, publishing relatively few articles in the established anthropological venues. (The major exception to this came in 1968 when he was invited to present proxemics as a research method in the journal *Current Anthropology*, where it was followed by critical responses from a handful of prominent researchers who rather condescendingly picked it apart.)[16] Hall was very self-conscious about the ways in which his sensibilities differed from other scientists. He articulated this difference as a matter of focus or perception. While most researchers concerned themselves with the "content" of communicational systems or the "functions" of gestures within those systems, he tended to see their "forms" and "structures."[17] Where most saw things, Hall saw relations. Where most could only see an isolated entity or event in space or time, Hall felt that he could perceive the warp and weft of space and time itself. Where others saw objects, Hall saw patterns. While other researchers self-assuredly isolated figures for observation, Hall was often mired in his own perceptual oscillation between those figures and their backgrounds.

Nonetheless, the mutual suspicion between Hall and the field of anthropology did not prevent his models of culture as "communication" from gaining traction. Indeed, Hall is primarily remembered today as a founder of the anthropological subdisciplines of nonverbal communication and intercultural communication.[18] Within Hall's larger project, proxemics occupies an ambiguous position, sometimes manifesting as a specialized subfield of the anthropology of communication and sometimes serving as a meditation on its preconditions. Historically, this ambiguity allowed proxemics to fall by the wayside while subsequent generations elaborated the more accessible category of nonverbal communication.

The other aspect of Hall's formation that prevented him from remaining comfortably within the academic confines of his discipline was his career trajectory, the eventfulness and intensity of which added to his work a palpable sense of social urgency. Hall continuously observed that globalization and urbanization were altering the patterns of culture, creating profound dissonance among people and their environments. This urgency would propel proxemics quickly past the theoretical stage and into an operative one. Hall occupied different professional and discursive positions simultaneously, caught among disparate disciplines and institutions with their own proxemic and linguistic codes. He found himself in front of congressional committees investigating the urban crisis, executives navigating international business relationships, or designers seeking data on the emerging category of human environment. His own career path reflected these vicissitudes, as he moved from government appointments to professorships, all the while serving as a private consultant to various constituencies.

After his military service and a brief foray into academics (including at Bennington), Hall spent the better part of the 1950s in Washington, DC, initially at the State Department's Point IV Training program, where he directed courses for diplomats going overseas.[19] Here, his work was ineluctably drawn into the military-industrial-research complex and a new world order that demanded ever more subtle forms of cultural sensitivity and nonverbal fluency. In this sense, he personified what Jennifer Light has described as a "defense intellectual."[20] But Hall tired of the politicking and McCarthyism at the State Department, and by 1956 he had found a research position at the nonprofit Washington School of Psychiatry. While there, he established his own consultancy called Overseas Training and Research, which provided services to corporate clients with business in foreign countries. This also marked the moment Hall's wife, Mildred, would become a more active participant in his professional and academic work. The Halls' research and business models were based on the idea that, in addition to learning the formal verbal and written forms of language, effective diplomats and businesspeople also needed to become conversant in nonverbal communication for different cultural settings.

Hall's movement through government, business, and academia is interesting, but it was hardly unique. Indeed, distinctions among these different worlds were collapsing at the time. Even after leaving Washington for the Illinois Institute of Technology in 1963, and taking up a purely academic research agenda, Hall would find himself imbricated in the machinations of the Cold War and domestic unrest alike. According to David Price, the CIA partially funded Hall's early work on proxemics via a cover NGO, the Human Ecology Fund.[21] Hall was unaware that his insights might be used for the 1963 CIA *Kubark Counterintelligence Interrogation* manual, but in retrospect, it is easy to see how the promise of a lexicon of human gesture and perception could have found any number of domestic and foreign political applications.[22]

The intelligence community would welcome Hall's 1959 book *The Silent Language* with great enthusiasm.[23] In this text, Hall drew from his years of overseas experience in the State Department, military, research, and business—having gained what he believed was substantial expertise in Japanese, Mediterranean, Arab, German, and British cultures—to elaborate a theory of cross-cultural nonverbal communication. The book was also a meta-statement on how anthropology would need to adapt to comprehend what were effectively invisible patterns of behavior, communication, and interaction at all levels of culture. In it, Hall signaled his reliance on biological theory as a kind of proof of the limits and universalities of human behavior. In his schema, however, culture was an "extension" of the organism that was not reducible to a biological baseline as in theories of sociobiology. He would also here offer some of the many examples of national and ethnic distinctions in nonverbal communication that would come to cast his work as reductionist and anecdotal—the punctuality of Mormons, the reticence of Germans, the touchiness of Arabs, the territoriality of American housewives, and on and on.

The fluidity with which Hall's methods and examples continuously slid from the biological to the cultural would suggest to many readers a relation of cause and effect between those categories, as opposed to one of mutual modification (which was closer to his intention). It is difficult to move from "every living thing has a physical boundary" to "like the Eskimo who has many different words for snow, the Arab has many different asking prices, each with a different meaning," without assuming some kind of motivated relation between the ethological generalization and the ethnographic example.[24] These paradoxes have relegated Hall to the status of an unsophisticated forerunner to disciplines that he is nonetheless credited as having pioneered.[25] Indeed, his lack of scientific rigor and theoretical sophistication were pointed out at the time. The British anthropologist Sir Edmund Leach described Hall as "a home-grown, very old fashioned, practical problem solving kind of American anthropologist" and poked fun at his cultural and ethnic stereotyping.[26]

But the relationship between proxemics and categories of identification such as nationality and race was far more intricate than these criticisms implied. In Hall's view, a fully implemented method of analyzing cultural patterns (with proxemics being one iteration of such a system) would be able to deconstruct the very category of "race" as a biological determinant. By quantifying spatial and communicational patterns, he sought data sets that could show how mechanisms of culture, rather than biology, produced subjects' realities. Those ethological realities Hall constantly relied on were species-specific for him; modifications beyond that level represented extensions of culture. Ostensibly perceivable racial and national patterns indicated a radically modified human environment, one that had produced bodies and minds that were both technologically overextended and trapped within spheres of perceptual limitation and communicational distortion.

His many travels notwithstanding, Hall's most intensive contact with these perceptual and communicational spheres came at two key moments in his professional development, both of which immersed him in the dynamics of superordination and subordination in Black-white power relations, and the harmful effects of urban segregation. The first of these experiences came during World War II when Hall was assigned to a Black Engineer General Service Regiment as orientation officer. Here, he realized that racism and cultural prejudice were not simply attitudes held by individual colleagues but were structurally embedded in the fabric of official procedure and communication. Recognizing that the materials used for soldiers' onboarding and service assignments made cultural assumptions that did not account for different social and ethnic backgrounds, Hall drafted his own unofficial versions for his men.[27] Twenty years later, from 1963 to 1964, Hall would conduct what was destined to be the only scientific experiments in proxemics with a number of African American subjects living on Chicago's South Side. He interviewed these subjects, recorded and photographed their behaviors, notated those behaviors, and then invited them to observe, record, and notate their own spatial and communicational realities. The protocol of these experiments, and its constant modification and subversion, pushed Hall's nascent proxemic notation system to its limits. Despite their lack of conclusive outcomes, these experiments indicated to Hall that inequality, bias, superordination, and other social dynamics were not simply a matter of personal sentiment or conscious intention; they had to be mapped across their environments. These power relations emerged from background conditions that few could perceive.

The ambiguous relationship between biology and culture in Hall's system would continually bedevil his work. Was he developing tools for finding organism-specific constants, for seeing past the distortions of cultural systems, or for elaborating the precise mechanics of those systems? Were these tools empirical or interpretive? Were his proper objects of study the stuff of psychology—to be found inside the subject's mind—or purely externalized as socially coded behaviors? Where were subjects located within these patterns? Were they users or merely conduits? Furthermore, were Hall's struggles with such questions evidence of his own methodological confusion, or was he bumping against the epistemological limits of (human) scientific method itself?

Whatever the case, these vicissitudes seem structurally related to Hall's hybrid intellectual development. He was, on the one hand, a pragmatist in the lineage of John Dewey and Charles Pierce. On the other hand, he was an early proponent of views that would come to be seen as "constructionist," part of a lineage running from his anthropological heroes Edward Sapir and Franz Boas to contemporaries such as Thomas Kuhn. The synthesis of these sources would lead Hall to believe in the paradoxical project of empirically verifying the actual mechanics of social construction as they operated in and on individuals and social groups. In the case of proxemics, Hall wished to trace microspatial phenomena that were seldom under the control of the subject, moments in which spatial relations carried the cultural structures that determined or constructed the individual or group's perception of reality and capacity to act in or on it.

The operative spatial logic here, of an action that takes place within a context or against a background, is complicated. According to Berger and Luckmann, even in the simplest social interactions, "the two individuals are constructing a background [...] which will serve to stabilize both their separate actions and their interaction." This background—this externality—is then reimposed or re-projected, its origins forgotten: "Only at this point does it become possible to speak of a social world at all, in the sense of a comprehensive and given reality confronting the individual in a manner analogous to the reality of the natural world."[28]

This reality must also be internalized, and this was another aspect of social and psychological dynamics that interested Hall. *"Experience is something man projects upon the outside world as he gains it in its culturally determined form,"* he wrote.[29] In this regard, his system resembles that of Georg Simmel. Both men were interested more in the quasi-realities of the *forms* of social relations than their contents. Simmel proposed a model whereby externalities were more responsible for internal affects or intentions than vice versa—where, once established, attributes such as "faithfulness" gained a kind of determinative autonomy.[30] Simmel's tracking of these concerns via social distance and bodily extension anticipated Hall's project in many ways: "the bodily proximity and narrowness of space makes the mental distance [of the urban crowd] only the more visible." And: "Man does not end with the limits of the body or the area comprising his immediate activity. Rather is the range of the person constituted by the sum of effects emanating from him temporally and spatially."[31] Berger and Luckmann noted the connection between Simmel's and Hall's "sociology of the body," in which "expressivity, gait and gesture are socially constructed."[32]

Proxemics could therefore be historicized as part of a nascent "sociology of space" and a subsequent spatial turn that rippled across many disciplines in the postwar decades. Indeed, Hall's work would inspire many other initiatives within anthropology and sociology that sought to understand space as discrete from time, for instance.[33] Hall's recognition that space had a distinct and palpable impact on subjectivity might even be connected to the contemporaneous work of Michel Foucault, who identified the twentieth century's obsession with space as supplanting the historical consciousness of the nineteenth century.[34] Hall's concern with space was not altogether different from Foucault's many descriptions of the spatial instantiation of power and the withdrawal of those disciplinary mechanisms from the consciousness of the individual subject. Similarly, proxemics might be viewed in parallel with Henri Lefebvre's theorization of the production of space in which space itself is seen as an active ideological agent ordering social relations.[35] While these connections to critical theory carry profound qualifications regarding their compatibility with proxemics as a science, the elaboration in France of *l'espace social* is entirely relevant to Hall's project. Indeed, as he was first exploring the idea of proxemics, Hall traveled to France and met with Paul-Henry Chombart de Lauwe, whose mapping of social movements in Paris would be a major influence.[36] Hall's work was not unknown in France; Roland Barthes alluded to proxemics in one of his late seminars, framing it as a poetic property of space itself: "proxemics: belongs to a typology of subjective spaces in that the subject inhabits them affectively [...] proxemical space: niche, nest. Which means, in a certain sense: (a) the space of your field of vision (or smell, or hearing), (b) where things get taken, where things get hidden, (c) where things are reached for, where things are touched."[37] Barthes's phenomenological understanding of proxemics may have overlooked its political aspects, but it helps us grasp the ways in which Hall's system was designed to quite literally map those locations where context or background made intimate contact with the perceptual and cognitive apparatuses of the subject.

In this regard, there is an even greater sympathy with the work of Pierre Bourdieu, who elaborated social space via the concept of *habitus*, in which "the disposition of agents, their habitus, that is, the mental structures through which they apprehend the social world, are essentially the product of the internalization of the structures of that world."[38] Once internalized, those literal and figurative structures are taken for granted as natural. Hall often found himself in a disciplinary position akin to Bourdieu's, in which he was obliged to repeatedly explain that in his analyses of social phenomena, his "emphasis has not been on either the manifest or even the latent *content* but rather on the structural details, the implicit perceptual elements."[39] In his famous book on photography (written at precisely the same time as *The Hidden Dimension*), Bourdieu describes that particular activity in terms of its conventionality and homogeneity when aligned with a particular class *habitus*. Less interested in the content of photography than in forms or structures of convention, Bourdieu would insist that photography was a privileged site of investigation for a sociology that sought to trace the internalization of external structures. This model of sociological enquiry endeavored "to establish how the myriad 'small perceptions' of everyday life and the convergent and repeated sanctions of the economic and social universe imperceptibly constitute, from childhood and throughout one's life, by means of constant reminders, this 'unconscious' which becomes paradoxically defined as a practical reference to objective conditions."[40] External structures are internalized and projected outward once again as backgrounds whose main function is to disappear. Hall was interested in the same "small perceptions" and how they were constituted by the traversal of environmental features and structures from the outside world to the inside world of the subject, where, once interpellated, they existed as out-of-awareness governors of perception and communication—as filters that (pre)determined what was perceived as reality itself.

But Hall would be unable to maintain Bourdieu's critical distance from certain types of images. Indeed, he would enter into a complex existential relationship with the photographic image and the graphical mark or notation. This engagement with both the production and interpretation of images correlated with a more direct engagement with space that would soon give rise to proxemics itself. Arguably the chapter that resonated most strongly with readers of *The Silent Language* was titled "Space Speaks"; in it, Hall first elaborated the image of the extended human territorial bubble as a communicational apparatus.

Perhaps the presence of spatial phenomena—their apparent concreteness and accessibility—promised a more tangible object of study for Hall. Backgrounds are everywhere, after all. Whatever the reasons, he began recording instances of human interaction that he witnessed during his everyday life and his many travels. It would later occur to him that these documents could be read and coded for different types of microspatial transactions—transactions he would soon begin to describe as proxemic.

The period immediately following the publication of *The Silent Language* would see Hall beginning to collect all manner of *visual* evidence for proxemic analysis. Between 1959 and 1966 or so, he developed the habit of always carrying a subminiature format Minox camera everywhere, snapping photos of strangers (and sometimes friends) in every conceivable public situation. The Minox is familiar to anyone who has watched spy movies from this period, as it always appears as a device for espionage, for the stealthy recording of secret files or enemy lairs. The shutter of the camera was integrated with its body construction, with one half of its rectangular volume sliding across the other to open the shutter and create an image. It is a striking irony that Hall unwittingly participated in CIA programs while consciously adopting some of their imaging techniques. Nonetheless, Hall was drawn to this particular piece of hardware for its convenience and discretion. It rested in a holster on his belt at all times, and he apparently became quite skilled at drawing it and quickly snapping surreptitious pictures of people.

The images were adequate, but possessed specific formal attributes that were inherent to the Minox format. Prints were small. Images tended to lack depth of field, and to be a bit washed out. They were grainy, for the most part, occupying a broad middle ground in the scale of black and white. But somehow this lack of visual resolution worked for rather than against Hall's methods. Something about their scale and uniformly washed-out surfaces begged for these little rectangular objects to be grouped and compared rather than to become singular objects of attention. Even the strips of microscopic negatives seemed to demand an eye that was constantly scanning rather than a focused and fixed gaze. In other words, they physically lent themselves to the type of pattern recognition on which proxemics was based.

But Hall's scanning eyes were not limited to the prints made by his spy camera. He was eager to have all manner of visual support for his emerging theory, and he happily accepted images made by others in any format. He cut out newspaper and magazine columns that had images of famous and anonymous subjects interacting. He saved hundreds of comic illustrations that he felt revealed various insights into these interactions. These shreds could be added to and mapped onto images of animals borrowed from fellow scientists. All of these pictures were obsessively analyzed and coded; their specific contexts, origins, and discursive purposes disregarded in favor of a kind of comparative superimposition of interactional patterns. This is not to imply that Hall was unaware of, or indifferent to, the disparate purposes or ideological modalities of these images. On the contrary, he was acutely aware of the subjective (conscious and unconscious) bias of both image production and interpretation, and he would invest a great deal of his energy in effacing that bias or corruption of data.

At this early stage, though, the images seemed an effective means of cataloging and illustrating the spatial communicational phenomena he had begun to describe in *The Silent Language*, in which he wrote:

> Every living thing has a physical boundary that separates it from its external environment. Beginning with the bacteria and the simple cell and ending with man, every organism has a detectable limit which marks where it begins and ends. A short distance up the phylogenetic scale, however, another non-physical boundary appears that exists outside the physical one. This new boundary is harder to delimit than the first but is just as real. We call this the "organism's territory." […] Man has developed his territoriality to an almost unbelievable extent.[41]

Could this overdeveloped territoriality—this hypertrophied background—be seen? Could it be measured and modeled via the instruments that allowed it to dilate, or the constraints it placed on subjects' bodies? Might it be possible to verify and quantify not just the conscious communicational contents of human interaction but the virtual frames, structures, and patterns generated by their movement into and out of the social subject? Hall conceived the patterns proxemics would soon describe as being generated from the individual in an outward movement but also directed at them, with cultural lines of force moving inward toward the ambiguous center of subjectivity. The field or surface at which these two directionalities met came to be figured by Hall as a kind of membrane—a second skin projected outward from the body surface but nonetheless constrained by the mechanisms of determination. There, hovering in this median space, was the boundary of a bubble. This boundary was a quasi-object that demanded its own method of description. It hung uneasily between biological laws and metaphorical projection, between constraining apparatus and extended field of affordance.

BUBBLES AND EXTENSIONS
This would be the work of proxemics, starting around 1960: to measure the surface tension of human boundaries and to chart their biological foundations and cultural extensions.[42] Hall conceived of his new method as a system to describe "how man unconsciously structures microspace."[43] Later, he would define proxemics as "interrelated observations and theories of man's use of space as a specialized elaboration of culture."[44] Before settling on this term, Hall had considered other neologisms such as "human topology, *chaology* (the study of boundaries), [and] *choriology* (the study of organized space)."[45] The methodological implications of this project were profoundly topological. Proxemics was not a simple compass that could trace a stable existential arc around a predefined subject. Rather it became an exercise in identifying the boundaries of the subject, tracing the flows of intentionality, perception, and interpellation as they worked their way between the shifting realms traditionally identified as of the interior and exterior worlds of that subject.

Hall's focus on the movements of these processes and patterns meant that his observations could not simply be limited to bodily comportment. After 1959, in particular, he became increasingly concerned with both the determinative and facilitative aspects of the physical attributes of the environment. He noted the degree to which architectural and urban spaces were understood as continuous or fragmented in certain cultures: Parisian streets, for instance, could be disorienting to outsiders, as the same thoroughfare might change names several times. He recalled that many of his State Department Point IV trainees reported feeling isolated in Latin America because of the architectural convention of the high wall separating the household courtyard from the public street. American offices were typically organized according to an evenly spaced grid, or what Hall saw as an all-over pattern in which everyone felt they had a proper place, whereas French offices were centralized and hierarchical with the size and placement of rooms in the plan determined by company rank.

Some cultures queued up at a ticket window in an orderly fashion while others crowded around it. Hall's examples moved from the urban scale to the bodily, with patterns constantly shifting from one environment to the next. In all of these, the subject was ensconced and constrained—always manipulating or conforming to a desk, a sidewalk, or other individuals.

Hall's attempts to accommodate spatial organization into his theories of intercultural communication developed across a series of papers published between 1960 and 1963, where the coinage "proxemics" first appeared. With titles such as "The Language of Space," "Architecture and Mental Health," and "Spatial Features of Man's Biotope," Hall seemed to be testing what a comprehensive human-environment observation method might include.[46] Also of note are the venues for these early papers: "A System for the Notation of Proxemic Behavior" appeared in *American Anthropologist* in 1963, just a few months after "Quality in Architecture—an Anthropological View" was published in the *Journal of the American Institute of Architects.*[47] But even as Hall's work appeared in these distinct discursive realms, his approach was never so neatly compartmentalized. Addressing the anthropologists, for instance, he cited the work of biologist Heini Hediger, art theorist Alexander Dorner, painter Maurice Grosser, and urban planner Kevin Lynch as sources of proxemic models.

Hall knew most of these theorists personally. He had met Dorner at Bennington in the 1940s—visiting and guest lecturing in his classes—at the time Dorner was completing *The Way Beyond "Art,"* a foundational text in postwar aesthetics.[48] As mentioned earlier, in 1961 and 1962 Hall traveled to Europe where he began a friendship with Hediger, then director of the Zurich zoo. In 1962, Hall gave the Leatherbee lectures at the Harvard Business School, and he took advantage of his time in Cambridge to meet with Lynch, who was working on his own spatial "experience notation" system.[49] It was clear from these contacts that Hall was desperately seeking information on not only human behaviors and their sources but also the perception and recording of those behaviors.

Indeed, one of the most fundamental challenges for proxemics was data collection, which was hampered both by the ubiquity, and obscurity, of this data. Because proxemics was oriented toward people's everyday interactions with the world around them, it was difficult to study in a laboratory setting. It involved out-of-awareness interactions, so informants could not simply be interviewed about their intentions and gestures. As a device for measuring pattern, proxemics could not even be used to speculate about the communicational contents of said gestures. It was not devised to answer the question "What do people *mean* when they behave in *x* manner?" Rather, it asked, "How does *x* behavior function as an index of cultural determination" (or social construction)?

These methodological complexities notwithstanding, Hall arrived at a minimal program for quickly notating what he believed to be the eight basic scales, or "proxemes," of human interactions in environments:

1 postural—sex identifiers
2 sociofugal—sociopetal orientation (sfp axis)
3 kinesthetic factors
4 touch code
5 retinal combinations
6 thermal code
7 olfaction code
8 voice loudness scale[50]

The notation system was meant to quantify meaningful variations of the irreducible units of bodily and perceptual interactions of subjects among themselves and with their surroundings. Did people face one another, and at what distance? Could physical contact occur if desired? Was regular eye contact maintained? Could the heat of the other's body be felt, or their smell be registered? Further, what consistencies emerged when these phenomena were recorded for large numbers of people? Did patterns appear that could be linked to specific ethnicities or genders? All of these variables were assigned pictographic and numerical values. Hall intended the pictographs to be used initially; once those were memorized, number values would be favored for efficiency and eventual computer input. This digitization would prove efficacious as the number of proxemes eventually increased to nineteen.

As a coding system, proxemics was a hybrid method partially based on weather mapping codes that Hall used in World War II, the grammatical trees of traditional linguistics, and other schema. Most significant were body movement notation systems. These were not new by 1960, of course. They have a long history intimately bound to models of the modern subject and various imaging technologies. From Eadweard Muybridge's photographic motion studies to Laban movement analysis, new methods for capturing, isolating, and describing human bodily movement were developed in the late nineteenth and early twentieth centuries. Systems like Étienne-Jules Marey's and, later,

Frank and Lillian Gilbreth's have a complex relationship to industrial modernity and its demands for a subject better suited to a machine environment. They were always already both documentary and operative, recording the way the body moves so that the same body could be conditioned to new types of interactions and environments. Proxemics can certainly be aligned with this Taylorist legacy, but Hall's media and imagery never really resembled its practice of situating objectively isolated bodies in framed and gridded spaces, showing discrete limbs performing repeated actions. Nonetheless, Hall's work is ergonomic in the sense that he was concerned with a particular kind of "fit" between subjects and the world.[51]

Also, Hall certainly would have been aware of the ethnographic origins of such recording systems, such as Franz Boas's frustrated attempts to film and systematically analyze the dances of the Kwakiutl people around 1930. Here was an instance in which photographic media was destined to be synthesized with formal notation (perhaps Labanotation) for the cultural analysis of various sorts of human "motor habits."[52] The outcomes of Boas's project would have been for cultural "salvage" and used to support his claims against biological determination. Though Hall's concerns were not historical, or necessarily even documentary, the parallel with Boas is noteworthy; in both instances the pictorial media and the notational system converged in an overdetermination of objectivity.

A similar overdetermination emerged in the work of Hall's Columbia colleague and fellow traveler Ray Birdwhistell. Birdwhistell's notational system for bodily movement—kinesics—was developed in parallel with Hall's assonant proxemics.[53] Kinesics is an important touchstone, not simply because it was a notational system but because it was an epistemological meditation on human "context." Birdwhistell's work with Gregory Bateson demonstrated that human behavior could not be isolated for study, just as human communication could not be understood as discrete words with internal meanings.[54] Hall would have agreed with Birdwhistell's observation that "a human being is not a black box with one orifice for emitting a chunk of stuff called *communication* and another for receiving it."[55] Instead, kinesics attempted to chart an emergent subject interacting with others, and with the physical features of the world around them.

Kinesics and proxemics were systems of behavioral "microanalysis" that used notation to tame the complexities of responsive and environmental situations by reducing them to a series of quantities and pictograms.[56] There was a certain family resemblance in their line drawings, tracking on notepads the complexities of human interaction in time. Both systems grew more complicated as they aimed to record increasing levels of complexity within interactions. There was always a factor to be identified (and notated) in between isolates, always a kind of dilation and pulling apart of phenomena into more and more component parts. The closer one looked, the more time seemed to slow; a simple gesture extended into an infinite poem of stimulus and response at the finest levels of granularity. Unsurprisingly, both kinesics and proxemics would fall into the pit of their own visual resolution.[57]

At the same moment that the notational apparatuses of microanalysis were emerging, architectural and urban design disciplines were also feeling the allure of a simplified alphabet of experience. As Hall refined his notational system, Kevin Lynch was creating a method that could account for subjects' awareness of their surroundings. Though not a notational system properly speaking, Lynch's mental maps were graphical or schematic representations of human-environment interaction. It was architect Philip Thiel who would provide a proper score for such interactions, what he described as a sequence-experience notation."[58] Thiel designed his incredibly ambitious system to account for the phenomenological aspects of architectural interaction through time. He hoped his method could become a simulation apparatus for designers to quickly try out combinations of spatial elements without having to execute detailed drawings or models. But, much more than just an expedient, Thiel's system was also a belated avant-garde attempt to align human perception with the unprecedented conditions of an emerging modern environment. Inspired by Gyorgy Kepes and James J. Gibson (also an important touchstone for Hall), Thiel was describing not just a new tool for designers but a new kind of human spatial experience, one characterized by simultaneity and technically and aesthetically dynamic models of interaction.

Perhaps closer to Hall's sensibilities, though, was the work of landscape designer Lawrence Halprin and choreographer Anna Halprin, with whom he worked on occasion. Lawrence Halprin's practice of "scoring" in urban space was similar to Hall's method in that it notated movements through the environment, but it was more prescriptive in the sense that it was capable of dictating actions to performers and participants within those environments. These newly programmed interactions might alter subjects' relationships to their environment and, in the process, shift the power dynamics inherent in those relationships. The two systems shared a presumption about the invisibility of human environment and the ways in which backgrounds were conditioning mechanisms. They also had in common an ethical presumption about the efficacy of raising subjects' awareness of those environmental mechanisms. Halprin, however, seemed content with simply drawing participants' attention to their own subjective responses in the novel situations he orchestrated. In one urban interaction piece, for instance, Halprin directed participants to visit particular spaces and make observations. They would then respond to questions such as: "How did you like riding the subway? Did you like the people on the subway? How do you think the other people on the subway felt about you?"[59] By contrast, a survey asking for direct subjective accounts would have been inadequate for proxemics; Hall would have interpreted the complex social interactions on a subway ride as already determined and dictated by out-of-awareness territorial and perceptual apparatuses.

Of all of these attempts to record or prescribe bodily comportment in social or literal space, proxemics was the most ambitious, and most problematic. Its failure, however, was not just due to its impossibly comprehensive scope but, more precisely, because of its positionality. Unlike Labanotation or kinesics, proxemics was not simply a way to codify the movements of a human body, nor was it, like the projects of Lynch, Thiel, or the Halprins, a way of describing that body's movements through space or the properties of the spaces themselves. Rather, it positioned itself in between these categories—in the space of interaction between bodies, between bodies and spaces, between figures and grounds.

This ambiguity of position is belied by the image of the bubble, which is all too easily understood as a stable sphere comprising bodily gestures and social mores (or something like "personal space").[60] In Hall's conception, the bubble was much more present and active than this metaphorical projection. Hall viewed the proxemic bubble as the interface for all human-environment interaction. It determined the field of activity of the subject, just as it filtered sensory data. It dictated what reached—and what could be reached by—the physical, perceptual, and cognitive faculties of the individual. It conditioned what could be understood and communicated. The bubble was the expanding and contracting surface at which social structures (backgrounds) made contact with the individual subject, where the virtual architectures of social life were internalized and projected outward once again.

The bubble was the quasi-real apparatus that allowed Hall to form his intuition that "people brought up in different cultures live in different perceptual worlds."[61] If the physical attributes of spaces and objects conditioned perception, then the cultural attributes of habit and convention could be just as determinative. Hall came to see perception itself as just as much an artifact of social construction as its instrument. Somehow, culture was conditioning not only behaviors and communication but the ability to perceive reality itself. Hall wrote: "There is a growing accumulation of evidence to indicate that man has no direct contact with experience per se but that there is an intervening set of patterns which channel his senses and his thoughts."[62] These references to patterns, channels, and (elsewhere in Hall's work) filters and frames were not mere metaphors. They were quasi-material structures—like the bubble—in which the subject was suspended, and through which that same subject acted in the world. In this sense, proxemics was a system not just for describing behaviors but for tracing the architectures of perception.

Another of Hall's concepts would prove relevant to fulfilling these ambitions. This was the idea of human "extensions." Extensions were technological objects or systems that augmented the innate capacities of the human organism to move, manipulate objects, perceive the world, and communicate. The theoretical elaboration of extensions would occupy Hall for the same period that he was working on proxemics. Extensions paralleled proxemics by theorizing the ways human territoriality was being expanded. If proxemics described a delimiting bubble, the notion of extension—a less well-developed concept—described an attenuated humanity, stretched beyond the limits established by nature. Hall had begun to think along these lines as early as *The Silent Language*:

> Today man has developed extensions for practically everything he used to do with his body. The evolution of weapons begins with the teeth and the fist and ends with the atom bomb. Clothes and houses are extensions of man's biological temperature-control mechanisms. Furniture takes the place of squatting and sitting on the ground. Power tools, glasses, TV, telephones, and books which carry the voice across both time and space are examples of material extensions. Money is a way of extending and storing labor. Our transportation networks now do what we used to do with our feet and backs. In fact, all man-made material things can be treated as extensions of what man once did with his body or some specialized part of his body.[63]

Whether manifested as a satellite, a park bench, or language itself, extensions offered Hall an evident connection between a subject's external reality and their internal states and perceptual capacities. This is certainly how Marshall McLuhan interpreted the idea in the early 1960s.[64] Indeed, McLuhan's adoption of the term (most famously in 1964's *Understanding Media: The Extensions of Man*) was inspired by the passage quoted above, which McLuhan rapturously referred to in his many letters to Hall as "your page 79."[65] In a 1964 letter, McLuhan would go even further: "to say that any new technology or extension of man creates a new environment is a much better way of saying the medium is the message."[66] Hall (before bequeathing it to McLuhan) gleaned the word from Buckminster Fuller. Fuller used the term "extension" as early as 1938: "Through the leverage gained by his INANIMATE INSTRUMENT EXTENSION OF SELF, [man] has attained an extended mechanical ability far in excess of his own integral mechanical and energy content ability."[67] As this passage suggests, Fuller took the entirely optimistic view that technology could only amplify the human capacity to self-actualize.

But McLuhan and Hall would offer alternative perspectives. In their view, extensions always had a reciprocal component. They turned back on the organisms they extended; they stunted, ablated, amputated, and distorted the senses they seemed to extend, as well as those they apparently did not affect. For every "outering," to use McLuhan's terms, there was also an "innering."[68] For his part, Hall wrote that "a species, once it begins to use the environment as a tool, sets in motion a whole series of new and often unforeseen environmental transactions that require further adjustments."[69] Hall, relying on Freud, essentially pathologized this cultural and biological condition, describing it as "extension transference," a process wherein the subject attributed the powers of the extension to themselves, further confusing the proper scales and domains of humanity and technology.[70]

This model of transference might allow us to revisit the ways that both proxemics and the theoretical model of extensions were, for Hall, modes of describing out-of-awareness behaviors and perceptual phenomena. In both instances, as humans either lost track of their innate capacities and allowed themselves to be stretched and anaesthetized or allowed their cultural-spatial patterns to conflict with one another, they were unaware of these mechanics. Hall wrote to McLuhan about the ramifications of these inside-outside dynamics:

> The idea that the organization takes place outside of the organism in visual and other fields is, I believe, thoroughly sound, albeit revolutionary. We have always labored under the impression that the organization was done by man himself, inside as it were. I see no evidence for this that will stand up. What I think happens is that the organization takes place outside and then becomes internalized as a solution, or solutions to a given category of contexts, and is later projected outward when one of these contexts triggers a

response. I think that H. S. Sullivan was trying to get at something like this, also that this is what Worff [*sic*] is talking about. Not only that culture is the sum of the external internalized patterns which man uses as a basis for organizing his behavior. There are certainly those which go on inside the person, all emotional responses, for example. But culture provides the link with the outside world.

I have noted from time to time that there is also another process at work in life which seems to balance the extensive, or ablative process and that is the internalizing process. One of the best examples that I can think of is in the case of the temperature control mechanisms. Internalization leads to greater flexibility and control—severs the bond with the outside world so that life can now move through rather than be contained in the environment. [...] I do not think that man has yet internalized his culture in this sense, that is man is imprisoned by what he does not know, particularly the out-of-awareness patterns of culture. It may be that people are afraid to see culture for what it is because while they will have escaped the controls, they will then have to take the responsibility of moving positively on their own. This in turn will lead to more extensions and ablations; we have no idea what these will be.[71]

"*So that life can now move through rather than be contained in the environment.*" This is a fascinating inflection point in a series of thoughts still too fluid for Hall to commit to print. It speaks to the larger ethical project of proxemics, which was to code the movements and embodiments of culture so that they might be transcended, or— and this is simply the inverse movement—so that they might be assimilated internally (like biological temperature control mechanisms) and incorporated into a new model of subjective agency in a world transformed by technological extensions and new social structures, or human bubbles.

Hall would explicate these proxemic dynamics most famously and influentially in his 1966 book *The Hidden Dimension*. This text, based on the previous six years' research into spatial phenomena, would secure Hall's reputation as an environmental design specialist (or at least a consultant to that field) and would launch the term "proxemics" into public and scientific consciousness. Instead of offering an account of specific techniques, however, *The Hidden Dimension* established the philosophy of proxemics. It grounded it in ethology and expanded it to a comprehensive theory of culture. The book begins with discussions of territoriality, and implications of overcrowding in animal populations, then moves to the sensory perception of space and ends with several cross-cultural proxemic analyses.

Hall includes two lengthy discussions of biological experiments: a study of deer populations on James Island in Maryland by John Christian and, more famously, John B. Calhoun's controlled study of rats conducted in a barn in the town of Rockland, Maryland.[72] Both studies revealed that overcrowding had implications beyond simply affecting the availability of food (the Malthusian doctrine). In both instances, as populations swelled, biochemical and behavioral changes occurred in both the deer and the rats. Endocrine (and presumably stress) levels were measurably higher, which led to erratic behavior and death.

In Calhoun's pens, crowding induced the rats to deviate from most normal patterns involved with mating, social hierarchies, and feeding. At a certain point, when the population density rose high enough, Calhoun described a "behavioral sink": "the outcome of any behavioral process that collects animals together in unusually great numbers. The unhealthy connotations of the term are not accidental: a behavioral sink does act to aggravate all forms of pathology that can be found within a group."[73] Here, it appeared to Hall, was ethological proof for the problems of the inner city and the failures of modern housing projects, to name only the most obvious examples.

Tom Wolfe also made these connections when he spent time with Hall for a *New York* magazine article in 1966:

> I just spent two days with Edward T. Hall, an anthropologist, watching thousands of my fellow New Yorkers short-circuiting themselves into hot little twitching death balls with jolts of their own adrenalin. Dr. Hall says it is overcrowding that does it. Overcrowding gets the adrenalin going, and the adrenalin gets them hyped up. And here they are, hyped up, turning bilious, nephritic, queer, autistic, sadistic, barren, batty, sloppy, hot-in-the-pants, chancred-on-the-flankers, leering, puling, numb—the usual New York, in other words, and God knows what else.[74]

In Wolfe's report, standing with Hall and looking down into Grand Central was very much like Calhoun looking into his rat pens in Rockland:

> The floor was filled with poor white humans, running around, dodging, blinking their eyes, making a sound like a pen full of starving rats or something.

"Listen to them skid," says Dr. Hall.

He was right. The poor old etiolate animals were out there skidding on their rubber soles. You could hear it once he pointed it out. They stop short to keep from hitting somebody or because they are disoriented and they suddenly stop and look around, and they skid on their rubber-sole shoes, and a screech goes up. They pour out onto the floor down the escalators from the Pan-Am building, from 42nd Street, from Lexington Avenue, up out of subways, down into subways, railroad trains, up into helicopters...

They screech! And the adrenal glands in all those poor white animals enlarge, micrometer by micrometer, to the size of cantaloupes. Dr. Hall pulls a Minox camera out of a holster he has on his belt and starts shooting away at the human scurry. The Sink![75]

"You could hear it once he pointed it out." This was Hall's role, in a sense, to perceive the invisible structures and patterns filling cultural space, structures that few others could perceive.

But Wolfe's reduction of Hall's theories to the rather two-dimensional model of the behavioral sink (not to mention the reactionary language in his characterization of social pathology) missed the subtleties of proxemic analysis as it was developing at that moment. For, just as in his earlier book, Hall was eager to transcend the ethological truisms of organism-environment dependency in favor of a meditation on the ways culture had transformed those dependencies. In *The Hidden Dimension*, he proceeded with this task methodically, if not always consistently. After explicating the sink and other biochemical aspects of crowding in animal populations, he devoted several chapters to "the perception of space." Here, at his most McLuhanesque, Hall distinguished among the "distance receptors" of eyes, ears, and nose, and the more proximal systems of olfaction and touch. The proxemes he had established a few years before—of thermal sensation, or visual engagement, the aura of smell, and so on, found grounding in a theory of perception itself (which was largely indebted to the work of J. J. Gibson).

On a more general level, Hall used this opportunity to describe his vision of an anthropology of space, and how it would need to comprise an analysis of environment that accounted for its backgrounds and patterns as much as its physical composition. *The Hidden Dimension* outlined three proxemic attributes of the environment: "fixed-feature space," "semifixed-feature space," and "informal space." In Hall's formulations, "features" were not necessarily physical; they were combinations of obdurate things, and equally obdurate (or modifiable) patterns. Fixed-features referred, then, not only to walls and buildings that could not be moved but also to the cultural conventions that had dictated their position in the first place, for example the streets themselves, as well as the tradition of the Roman grid. Accordingly, semifixed features included furniture but also the interpersonal patterns of their use in different types of spaces—the proverbial park bench, its users positioning themselves on it relative to each other.

The last proxemic category Hall described was perhaps the most significant, primarily because of its insidious nature: "I have called this category *informal space* because it is unstated, not because it lacks form or has no importance. Indeed [...] informal spatial patterns have distinct bounds, and such deep, if unvoiced, significance that they form an essential part of the culture. To misunderstand this significance may invite disaster."[76] Informal space was effectively another rendering of the personal space bubble. It was not physically "fixed" as an obdurate "feature," but Hall nonetheless wished to stress its reality. It may not have been material, but it certainly had form. Informal space was made from culturally conditioned patterns, gestures, and sensorial filters. In this sense it seemed to subsume the other categories of spatial features. It was the field comprising the city, its physical fabric of streets, buildings, and open spaces, down to its smallest structuring elements—the heights of curbs, tightly packed café tables under a striped awning, the size of the window that the bank teller sat behind, or a cluster of office chairs at the end of a conference table. It was the park bench awaiting the lunch hour when office managers, secretaries, and janitors (all potentially from different cultural backgrounds) would sit for a few minutes, adjusting their posture, fixing their gazes, inching their bodies toward or away from their neighbors.

As was so often the case in Hall's work, these profound environmental insights failed to lead to rigorous critical analyses, ending instead with reductive and cliched cultural anecdotes about human bubbles and extensions. "Germans sense their own space as an extension of the ego," he observed. The English are more reluctant to use phones than Americans, being more fearful of social "intrusions." (They also maintain more consistent eye contact during conversation.) The Japanese historically ordered their cities hierarchically from center to periphery. "Pushing and shoving in public spaces is characteristic of Middle Eastern culture."[77] And so the evidence moved, from bodily comportment to ego projections to the placement of desks and cash registers to the physical fabric of cities. Hall's theoretical musings never seemed to find explicit resolution, just as the proper object of study of proxemics never seemed to be isolatable. Nonetheless, Hall perceived a highly charged arena in which a subject was much more than an individual body within which sat a single consciousness. He conceived subjects as being possessed of nonmaterial endo- and exo-structures. Such structures extended subjects beyond the boundaries of their skins and simultaneously gathered and coalesced a tiny (predetermined) portion of the vast amounts of sense data in the environment. Just as surely as subjects sat on the bench, the bench was working on them, conditioning their bodies and orienting their sensory apparatuses, allowing them or forcing them into different patterns of proximity and communicative potentiality relative to others.

How to *see* this field? To trace its contours, to perceive the infinite moiré of its overlapping lines of human and nonhuman force? What would a notated and aggregated body of data regarding these patterns reveal about humanity and its relationship to the apparatus known as the social? Once perceived, could these mechanisms be escapable? By placing them into human awareness, might we be able to transcend or internalize these social mechanisms in order to be able to "move through" a newly conceived environment instead of simply being "contained within" it? Such was the impossible task Hall set for his proxemic method—a method grounded in empiricism but whose existential and metaphysical ambitions could not be denied.

AT IIT

If at some point Hall had intended *The Hidden Dimension* to be a summary or codification of proxemics, it was evident by the time it was published that it would not serve that goal. Indeed, it barely mentioned the intensive research he had been conducting as he had been writing (1963–66). The book instead gathered his less formal explorations in human-environment interaction from three years prior, when he was traveling to Europe. These recollections were coupled with an overview of the various levels of environmental "features" that might be considered in an anthropology of space. Together, these two aspects of the book feel preliminary to Hall's new science yet like an elaboration of its metaphysical ramifications. At no point does the idea of proxemics emerge as a central object of elaboration. Even Hall's compulsive visual production did not find adequate representation in the book. There are several photographs juxtaposing animal and human groupings and a few diagrams of spatial principles, but the thousands of coded images in Hall's filing cabinets remained hidden away, their subtleties presumably too elusive for the lay reader.

These were subtleties Hall had become intimately familiar with as he assumed his position at the Illinois Institute of Technology in Chicago in 1963. His return to academics signaled a kind of official acknowledgment of the severity of the inter-ethnic and intercultural problems proxemics sought to address. At least for a moment, it seemed that proxemics might be able to quantify social tension writ large, that it might have the ability to cut through the particularities of domestic unrest and global uncertainty. In the fall, Hall arrived on campus as a key hire in the new Liberal Studies program, which was intended to serve several departments but most particularly the Institute of Design.[78] With grant funds from the National Institute of Mental Health—for conducting research on the "Ethnic Use of Micro-Space in Interethnic Encounters"—and the Human Ecology Fund, he established a laboratory of sorts and hired assistants for different data-gathering initiatives, field work, and developing a coding system for computer input and processing. He called these three stages "phenomenological, phenomenal, and statistical," referring to the experiences of subjects, the recording processes of observers, and the aggregation of data.[79] The final aspect of this work was the founding of a Proxemics Research Center at IIT in 1965 (though the structure and activities of this center are murky).[80]

A careful look at the work Hall did at IIT is instructive, as it gives a better sense of the social and racial stakes of his project, and the aesthetic, political, and scientific complexities out of which it was formed.[81] A fairly complete record of this moment is found not only in the archive but also in Hall's *Handbook for Proxemic Research*, published in 1974. The foundation of this work emerged when Hall learned of a community service program in Chicago's South Side. Serving the local African American community, the Isham YMCA had begun a job interview training program. Participants were African Americans (most of whom had not finished high school) who were being trained in specific job skills. (Hall would designate these subjects "working-class blacks," or WCBs.) They also learned interview skills, which would become Hall's area of focus. He suspected that the subjects' frustration with the job market was not solely due to a lack of skills or experience but also not entirely reducible to overt bias and racism (though they were certainly factors). For Hall, a major component—and possibly structuring these other factors—was the role that incompatible proxemic bubbles played in the interview process between those seeking positions, and their (inevitably) white interviewers. To test this hypothesis, Hall and several student assistants (most from the IIT design program) set up a model office in which to rehearse interviews with volunteers from the program. Interviews were recorded, photographed, and filmed (although none of the footage survived). These records were then used for proxemic coding.

The interactions that took place in Hall's modest interview office would be the first chance to test, replicate, and verify the methods of proxemics. What had until then been an intuitive process that Hall conducted on his own in informal field situations would finally be subjected to scientific rigors. In actuality, verification would be elusive. To begin with, Hall would not pursue a recognizable object of observation. He was not analyzing speech or even body postures per se, but rather the textures of interaction that took place between an ever-changing (even in this controlled situation) ensemble of actors—interviewer, interviewee, and environment. Here, Hall's perennial problem of identifying the isolates that proxemics was meant to decipher would bedevil his attempts to establish the basic units of what he and his assistants were attempting to observe. He would become more and more sensitive to the conditioning mechanisms of the scientific apparatus itself. In other words, he could not help but to become aware of the proxemic limitations of those conducting interviews, taking photographs, and writing notations. In a certain sense, his original focus on these disadvantaged subjects would be reframed as an agonistic meta-analysis of the paradigm of the human sciences. The nuances of this transition are worth pausing over because they constitute a moment at which the production of social (and racial) knowledge was highly mediated by considerations that might best be characterized as aesthetic. Hall's experiment dealt with the problem of observing and formally describing not just invisible territorial bubbles but the oscillation of figure-ground relationships within a particular environment, perceptual framing and filtering on the part of subjects and researchers, and the recognition of patterns in a mass of ambiguous data.

The interview seemed straightforward enough. Subjects entered the room, introduced themselves to the interviewer, then proceeded to answer questions about their professional experience and personal background. The questions themselves were really a feint, however. Hall was not interested in *what* subjects and interviewers were saying but in *how* they were saying it through their microspatial behaviors and manipulation of environmental extensions. The stated objects under observation were the proxemes of Hall's system—bodily distance, eye contact, relative body position (direct or oblique), and so on. Additionally, Hall and his assistants sought indices of tension and relaxation. What behaviors or environmental factors might put the subject at ease rather than elicit apprehension? How could those affects be recognized?

Interviews were recorded on film and audiotape. While a "proxemicist" could simply have observed and notated the interview as it happened, Hall wanted records, presumably so that results could be replicated and illustrated citing the audiovisual evidence. But one of Hall's first challenges was finding the means of capturing this experiment. Filmed images were not of a sufficient resolution to be carefully analyzed. Still images provided the requisite detail but could not record second-to-second transitions among proxemic isolates. Hall settled on a Nikon F camera with a motor-driven exposure unit for 250 frame sequencing. This provided a near movie-like rate of capture in a high-fidelity visual form. The camera was mounted in a soundproof box in the office, while an observer sat just outside looking through a small window made of one-way glass in the door, with the shutter release in hand. The observer—initially Hall or one of his assistants, and later the subjects themselves—would determine when a meaningful transaction was taking place and photograph it.

The mise-en-scène of the office space received no less consideration than the recording techniques. Various desk-chair relationships were tried. Furniture was pushed against the walls or clustered in the center of the space. Lighting was adjusted. Hall even noted the age-old difficulty of photographing darker skin—a "problem" scholars have recently traced back to bias in the development of photographic technology itself.[82] This issue was solved by covering the desk with a bright white material to increase the amount of reflected light. The arrangement of the room was not simply a logistical problem or an expedient for optimal recording. Subjects' interactions with the space and its "semi-fixed features" were also under observation. The chairs might be arranged in a certain way initially, but proxemic dynamics seemed to cause both subjects and researchers to shift them during their encounters. Hall came to see the desk, for instance, as an intervening spatial element that conditioned behavior, implied a power hierarchy, and extended the bodies of participants.

It was difficult to assimilate the incredible complexity of these phenomena into the notation system. Hall would consider some of them to be peripheral to his main concerns, but they evidently nagged at him. In addition to bodily proxemes, Hall noted the manipulation of the office furniture:

Position of the applicant's chair—sometimes in a normal position and occasionally in a different, even awkward position—was marked before the interview. Thus, we could determine precisely how much, if any, it had been moved during the session. [...] This set of observations represents a sort of footnote to the main study, but it was revealing in that it confirmed an aspect of black behavior that had been previously observed, i.e., that the blacks with whom we were working were, when compared to most whites, extraordinarily sensitive to spatial arrangement. When an interviewee would enter the room it was observed that as he seated himself he would unconsciously align his chair with some other feature of the room, usually the side of the desk. Experimentally moving the chair out of line as little as 1/10th of an inch produced almost imperceptible [sic] precise realignment with the original object.[83]

Thus, metonymically, what Hall described as the "situational frames"— a phrase he used as a more formalized acknowledgment of the role of context in interaction—of proxemics were in continuous movement. These forms slid from the subjects' conscious or unconscious intentions outward to their bodily movements, extending once again to the physical objects around them, then focusing back once again to their sensorial bubbles—what they were able to perceive (or not). At times the subjects seemed to be manipulating microspace; at others it was clearly manipulating them.

Methods of recording and notating the interviews were no less slippery, as the proxemic minutia continually eluded consistent coding. The number of proxemes ballooned at times; on other occasions, they were abandoned in favor of seemingly simpler "semantic differentials" such as "bored/interested," "friendly/angry," and so on. Hall tried different methods to translate the data for computer input, eventually settling on a specially developed FORTRAN algorithm that could handle values regarding the coder, the subject, the location of recorded interactions, and the nature of those interactions. Hall established numerical values for eighty variables. These began with information about the coder, the documents (photographs and notations) they produced, and a timescale of the recorded interaction down to the hundredth of a second—this timing presupposed the future implementation of a film camera along with slow-motion playback into the process. These were followed by codes for location and setting, from country to park bench. The type of activity was recorded—its nature and the nature of the relationship of the interactants—followed by data on the interactants themselves, including ethnicity, sex, age, and social status. Finally, eighteen "proxetic" (or sensory) codes were input. Hall left blank spaces throughout the lists "in view of the need to add items later."[84] "The way I've set up the program," Hall wrote McLuhan, "is that one should be able to compare—using a computer—just about any transaction at any point in time at any place on the globe and the effect of the observer on that transaction, as well as the effect of the person who is coding the data on both of them. It's an elaborate program."[85]

Hall's qualification marked by the word "should" belied the challenges of notating and interpreting proxemic phenomena. Even after the office arrangement, recording equipment, and notational system seemed to be set, there were other variables for which to account. First and foremost was the problem of subjective variation on the part of observers. From the moment the interview began, the observer made decisions about when to release the camera shutter. These decisions were effectively structured by what was perceived as constituting an isolatable proxemic event or gesture. When did such gestures begin and end? When should the recording sequence begin and end? Even once those qualitative choices had been made, the resulting images still had to be coded, and those notations reviewed for accuracy. Predictably, different observers identified wildly different behavioral isolates and significant moments in the communicational transactions.

Through this work Hall began to conclude that culture was "distorting" every moment of not only the subjects' interactions but also the research conditions, assumptions, and procedures. His white and Black students perceived events differently; subjects identified others still. Unconsciously, observers used the camera and the notational process according to their own cultural patterns. A strange dilation then occurred. Within just a couple of months, Hall considered his student assistants to be part of the experiment (their behaviors noted and coded). Subsequently, Hall invited the subjects themselves to photographically record interviews and then analyze the resulting images and recordings.[86] While it is unclear exactly what Hall hoped to achieve through switching these roles, he felt that the photographs taken by subjects belonging to one ethnic or economic group were substantially different from those taken by his assistants. He claimed that the "working-class black" subjects could distinguish photos taken by other Black subjects from those taken by non-Black observers based purely on the formal properties of picture angle, framing, zoom, and so on.[87]

In this way, the work in Chicago might be considered alongside other critical considerations of the role of photography and film in anthropology—by Gregory Bateson and Margaret Mead or, later, Paul Byers and John Collier.[88] Hall came to understand the photograph not simply as a record but as a "releaser" of observational activity, an "elicitor," as Collier might have said, of insight.[89] But whereas the traditional understanding of anthropological photo-elicitation involves the use of photographs with informants or interviewees, Hall folded that phenomenon of release back onto the observational method.[90] For him, the images helped to make his assistants aware of their own unconscious limitations and allowed subjects to *see* things that had previously been invisible. Hall began to perceive a possible anthropology of photography itself, wherein what are normally considered the formal attributes of the medium—frame, zoom, the moment (decisive or otherwise) captured—were all subject to proxemic constraint and extension.

But even this level of self-reflexivity would prove inadequate to overcome how the proxemics of seeing and photographing disrupted the observation of the interviews. For the recording media themselves were always imposing their own constraints and socially constructed frames. This state of affairs might have produced an opportunity for a postmodernist meditation on the ontic instability of images. Instead, Hall viewed these subjective limitations as obstacles to imagistic objectivity.[91] This prompted him to subject the photographs themselves to peculiar proxemic modifications. Hall noted that peripheral factors— the table on which an image rested and the features of the room, for instance—impinged on one's ability to see a standard-sized print clearly (not to mention one's instilled cultural biases). Even when projected in a darkened room, the distance between the observer and the projection screen seemed too great and disruptive. For this reason Hall designed and constructed a special viewing apparatus using a projector and a rear projection screen to magnify and place the filmic image as close to observers as possible, allowing them "to make full use of foveal vision," to avoid distraction and project themselves fully into the filmic space.[92] This device, which at first glance was a rather elementary assemblage of film equipment, ground glass, and aluminum struts, was in reality an apparatus designed to transcend perceptual bias. It was intended to pull observing subjects so close to the recorded document that they could penetrate their own culturally patterned screens.

As these technical, aesthetic, and racial dynamics were playing out in Hall's laboratory, he continued his field photography, seeking out groups and crowds of people (often with Black and white people together). For this purpose, he set up a mobile "blind" in a Hertz rental van that could be parked on the street unobtrusively. Inside, a research assistant used the Nikon F to capture groups at a distance. These "natural" scenes of interaction are undoubtedly disturbing for their imposition of a surveillance condition on subjects (although photographing people in public space was and is not uncommon in anthropological fieldwork); nonetheless, they represent Hall's attempt to explore the conditioning mechanisms of urban space. Buildings and infrastructural features frame these scenes in working-class, largely segregated neighborhoods, commercial signage and street furniture at times enlivening the otherwise monotonous walls and vast street intersections.[93] Hall was also afforded a privileged view into interior scenes of Black domestic life when one of his assistants—an African American IIT student named Marshall Williams—photographed friends in more intimate settings. (This series of images does not seem to have been systematically coded.)

Some of these Chicago images, and others taken around the same time, were subjected to other notational experiments. The most striking was a method of tracing images onto onionskin paper. The resulting red line drawings, which were absent of skin color and details of clothing, could be used to code interactions, presumably without the bias-inducing markers of race or class. These images allowed Hall to code the activities of larger groups, graphing multiple subjects together so that patterns might emerge.

Despite their different settings, all of these images constitute an intensive meditation on place. They are documents of bodily comportment and social interaction framed and grounded by specific environmental attributes. In the street scenes, mailboxes and shop windows ensconce subjects. In most instances some vertical element—a stop sign, a lamppost, a traffic light pole—acts as a social affordance. Individuals lean on, touch, or simply seem to gravitate toward these framing devices. They are environmental elements constantly used or avoided, but they seldom occupy the center of attention. These existential-magnetic attractions are far from mere conveniences; they are proxemic mediators and facilitators of all human relations. They instantiate space itself as a quasi-substance in which the subject is immersed and conditioned. The ground advances, and the figures are ever more intimately incorporated into it.

These optical, aesthetic, and political dynamics are all the more poignant given the palpable racial tensions in the streets of Chicago and across the United States in the 1960s. Proxemics had emerged out of a series of informal observations made abroad, and in Hall's own social circles, but its scientific validity was only truly tested in the charged space of the segregated city—shaped by and, in turn, shaping racial difference. Though Hall rejected the validity of race as a biological determinant, his attempt to map such determining mechanisms elsewhere—outside of the subject, and out of their awareness—was just as problematic in its reification of racial difference. The measuring of Black distance, the tracking of Black eye movements, of the Black manipulation of microspace, these were so many attempts to zoom in on the spatial dynamics of social construction, to part the curtain of cultural extensions, so to speak. But what did Hall expect to find beneath the taut surface of the personal space bubble? An exposed mass of organismic functions? An unguarded, universal human subject? This remains unclear, for this method of microanalysis, despite every device Hall employed to eliminate perceptual distance—switching the roles of observer and subject, observational blinds, special viewing apparatuses, drawing techniques, computer algorithms—remained mired in the middle ground of alienation and difference. Like the filmic dolly zoom Alfred Hitchcock had perfected just a few years earlier in *Vertigo* (1958), figures seemed to advance toward the viewer, but, in reality, a visual and spatial periphery was constantly expanding. The supreme irony in all of this was that proxemics could simply never get close enough.

ENVIRONMENTAL DESIGN

Science could never be satisfied in the anamorphic middle ground charted by proxemics. But design could. Indeed, design inhabits the space of extension and affordance that so fascinated Hall and many others at this moment. Accordingly, Hall's insights would intrigue the design establishment following the publication of *The Hidden Dimension*. Perhaps it was the virtuality of the bubbles he seemed to perceive—their tantalizing quasi-materiality—that made the anthropologist's patterns feel accessible. Here was an immaterial structure generated out of human interaction with the environment that was nonetheless carried around as a set of projected needs or factors. It was exactly what the emerging field of environmental design needed—traceable, tangible patterns of response. "If, however, one sees man surrounded by a series of invisible bubbles which have measurable dimensions, architecture can be seen in a new light," Hall wrote.[94] The "features" of the environment that informed the subject's proxemic range of movements were simultaneously extensions of that subject and part of the very fabric of their territorial bubble. In the same regard, buildings can be seen as both constraining frames and the outward projection of temperature control or bodily support (floors, walls, furniture) or designed elements. The site of conscious intervention on the part of governments, institutions, and individuals, the built environment presented a tangible setting for proxemic intervention, hovering at the border between subject and world.

But proxemics was not an anthropological method that was simply imported or translated into the disciplines of architecture and design. Rather, the history of Hall's elaboration of proxemics could be recounted as a parallel story to the anthropologist's interactions with architecture. This exercise would demonstrate that proxemics was not simply a method first theorized and then applied but was instead formed out of architectural and environmental questions to begin with. It is this acute circularity that is of particular interest here.

Hall's travels in Europe in 1961 and 1962 marked his initial forays into architecture and urban space as an object of research. During these trips, he met with Zurich zoo director Heini Hediger and other scientists but also with the French sociologist Paul-Henry Chombart de Lauwe and psychiatrist Paul Sivadon, an environmental design pioneer.[95] These meetings occurred as Hall was publishing some of the earliest statements on proxemics in the journal *Landscape*, which would begin to bring his work to the attention of designers.[96] He also visited Ernö Goldfinger in London, who shared articles from the 1940s regarding spatial sensation.[97] Hall wrote to Goldfinger in 1963 informing him of his new job: "I am moving to the scene of what's left of the Bauhaus—Illinois Institute of Technology—come Fall."[98] Once in Chicago, Hall's immersion in design culture only intensified. He was working with design students at IIT and forming contacts with architects in the city. His new neighbor was Bertrand Goldberg, and the two would go out for daily jogs, discussing urban and architectural issues. Hall worked with John Entenza to organize a series of lectures for the Graham Foundation on psychological and perceptual factors in architecture. By 1967, thanks to Marshall McLuhan's introduction, Hall would become a fixture of Constantinos Doxiadis's Delos cruises, which brought together architectural and government luminaries to discuss the world's crises in housing and urbanization. These years also saw Hall speaking at countless AIA meetings and architectural schools across the country. This list of contacts and affiliations is not meant as proof of Hall's architectural credentials so much as an indication of the dialogical nature of his engagement with the design establishment. He sought out architecture as much as it would seek him out. Designers needed method as much as Hall needed proof. For it quickly became apparent to Hall, as he turned his attention to space, that what seemed immediate and tangible—physical spaces and the arrangement of what he would soon describe as "features"—was actually incredibly hard to track.

Hall would find this out as he was working in his laboratory at IIT. Simultaneously, in 1964, he was hired as a consultant by Don

Emmons of Public Structures, Inc., consulting architect to Parsons Brinckerhoff-Tudor-Bechtel, a joint engineering venture working on the new San Francisco BART mass-transit system. Hall was referred to Emmons by architect Christopher Alexander who was the lead consultant on the human factors aspect of the design.[99] This would be one of the defining projects of what would come to be known by the end of the decade as "environmental design." Alexander, in his typical fashion, had arrived at a kind of master list of behavioral patterns and usage requirements; this "List of 500" was then sent to researchers in New York, Chicago, Philadelphia, and Toronto, who were to conduct analyses of the transit systems in those cities. Hall was tasked with making observations of users of the Tech-35th and Monroe-State Street stations on the Chicago Transit Authority's (CTA) Cicero-Congress Street line.[100] Tech-35th was, conveniently, the stop at IIT, where Hall had recently begun his professorship. The List of 500 (which may have reached the high 700s at one point) is significant in its own regard as it asked for information that would soon come to be recognized as proxemic: "How far apart should people talking to one another be, at different noise levels?" "What makes people feel the illusion that they have enough space, even when it is less than they would tolerate under other conditions?" "Do people really care about other peoples' transistor radios?" "How near is 'not touching'?"[101]

Hall and his students were deployed to the stations, where they determined peak load times during rush hours, made observations, and interviewed passengers and station attendants. They noted each subject's role (passenger or employee), sex, age, ethnic affiliation, and socioeconomic status. Interview data was paired with observation of nonverbal activity: where passengers tended to group while waiting, the degree to which they were willing to touch or shove one another to make it on the train, how the cold air affected circulation on the platforms and trains, and how immediately they took a seat when it was available.[102] Race and gender-inflected proxemic bubbles came into view as well. Hall noted that some activities required "at least" five square feet of space around individuals—buying tickets, purchasing concessions, reading newspapers (for males), and carrying packages, but he observed that men generally took up more space than women. Some observations seemed self-evident—the elderly and infirm were the first to utilize seats. Others strike us as more problematic—Black passengers seemed to want more warmth than white passengers and were observed grouping around the heating stoves on the platforms. Hall and his team noted crowding patterns during loading and unloading, conversational distances, and volumes of passengers in the train and on the platform. They attempted to record psychological phenomena such as boredom or claustrophobia, the perceived ease of navigating the system, getting help when needed, and feeling secure in the lonelier stretches of the stations.

Hall's written report was both observational and prescriptive. He researched seat design and arrangement in other systems. He wrote descriptions of passenger behavior and drew plans of the platforms showing structural features and furniture, as well as the body orientation of passengers. (He even proffered his own design for a three-sided column that would accommodate a single leaning body in a visually protected field.) There was a huge variety of classes of data, running from individual users' emotional responses to the physical features of trains and architecture. It was demographic, statistical, quantitative and qualitative by turns, and speculative. The report became a political indictment of the CTA as much as a set of utilitarian considerations for the BART. Hall perceived a circularity in the inadequate services and poor upkeep of facilities, and in the fact that only certain socioeconomic and ethnic groups used the Chicago system. Nonetheless, the report identified problems and offered design solutions in very general terms. Passengers might be made to feel more secure using the system, for instance, if maps were located at consistent points in all stations. Platforms should offer more seating, and the economical arrangement of seats on trains could alleviate proxemic intrusions (Hall did not use his neologism in his report). Turnstiles should be redesigned to alleviate congestion and make it easier for those carrying packages. Hall even suggested installing ultraviolet lamps throughout the system to combat germ transmission.

Variety notwithstanding, none of Hall's individual methods that winter were groundbreaking. It seems unlikely that his conclusions would have been received with a great deal of surprise. But the BART study marks an important historical moment just the same. In both Alexander's conception and Hall's characteristic response, we see a shifting design paradigm; one that posited user-generated behaviors as a source of design forms. Alexander would describe such behaviors in formal terms, as geometrical relations and patterns.[103] Others would increasingly describe them as new functional requirements for all kinds of buildings and design objects.

But such "requirements," which are always propositions about causes and effects, were hard to track. Even before he moved to Chicago, Hall had been seeking such correspondences. He asked all of his new design contacts for *examples* of the determinative mechanisms of the built environment, but he came away with only vagaries or anecdotes that could not satisfy his scientific sensibilities. In 1961, however, during meetings at the US Bureau of Standards, John D. Hoffmann told Hall about a failed research facility in upstate New York built by IBM.[104] Originally intended to spur creativity via the manipulation of rather quotidian parameters of room scale, lighting, and placement of offices relative to research spaces, the design ended up having the opposite effect. Perhaps, Hall thought, this instance where "architectural and human equipment were at odds with each other" could provide some evidence of correspondences between architectural arrangement and human behavior.[105]

For at least a year, Hall hunted for information about the building, his letters slowly working their way up the IBM leadership organizational chart. Finally, after many assurances of discretion and his good intentions, Hall received a report from Donald B. Miller, laboratory administration manager, regarding the infamous Building 701. Built in 1954 in Poughkeepsie according to the design of Voorhees, Walker, Foley & Smith, this facility proved dark, confining, and awkwardly composed in plan. Miller's account downplayed these drawbacks as wonderful learning opportunities, but it was apparent that the offices were strangely long and narrow, and hallways were insufficiently lit. Miller's letter was accompanied by office plans (of 701, and improved examples), and several Polaroids showing interior spaces. These documents, however, did not provide proof of any laws governing human-architecture compatibility. IBM had not discovered a motivated connection between environment and creativity. Nonetheless, it marks a micro-episode in the history of environmental design in which the immaterial aspects of the building advanced as objects of consideration. Room proportions, lighting, and placement of furniture were understood here not simply as fulfilling programmatic requirements but as facilitators of human response.[106] This particular explication was cultivated out of a novel disciplinary configuration: an anthropologist (at that moment a freelance consultant) at the Washington School of Psychiatry soliciting business and facilities managers for information about the human-environment interface.[107]

The idea that design should proceed from use patterns and human factors, and, further, that those patterns were visible and quantifiable, was new. Its impact was evident in the rapid formation at this precise moment of an ensemble of new disciplines, methods, and organizations devoted to the study and design of the human-environment relationship. The Environmental Design Research Association (EDRA) was founded in 1968. This organization grew from a series of British and American meetings and publications that were known as Design Methods, or the

Design Methods Group.[108] Major centers of environmental (design) research were established on both coasts in the United States and at several institutions in Europe. The Massachusetts Institute of Technology was perhaps the major epicenter, where the School of Architecture and Planning was turned toward the larger "social" issues of the period. Berkeley's College of Environmental Design was established earlier in 1959.[109] Christopher Alexander founded the Center for Environmental Structure there in 1967.[110] The Division of Man-Environment Relations in the College of Human Development at Penn State was also a major new program, and one intimately linked to founding members of EDRA. Another center for these activities was at the University of Utah, where the sociologist Irwin Altman opened up lines of communication between social scientists, psychologists, and architects beginning in the late 1950s. (Hall spent time at this program as well.) And while none of these initiatives resulted in anything like a specific, stable, and definable set of procedures that constituted a discipline, dozens more programs were established, departments merged, or social science faculty hired within or affiliated with architectural design programs.

Hall's appointment at IIT was a tentative step in this same direction, and proxemics emerged from his work there around 1965. However, Hall's method was not simply the product of a government-funded research project. Rather, it was simultaneously being elaborated as a commercial enterprise. During these same years, Edward T. Hall Associates continued to grow a client list, not solely in the international business sector but in the design fields as well. Perhaps more than any other approach to human-environment interaction, proxemics promised to bridge the epistemological and material divide between an understanding of human behavior and perception and the implementation of physical structures that might alter and ameliorate those behaviors and perceptions. In this sense Hall was a prototypical "human factors," "user experience," and ergonomics expert.

As a consultant, he began using concepts such as optimization, productivity, and user satisfaction. He ran workshops and brainstorming sessions, convened focus groups, conducted post-occupancy interviews, and lectured in professional settings on the importance of psychological and cultural factors in the built environment. By the end of the 1970s, Hall's client list included Skidmore, Owings & Merrill; Chloethiel Woodard Smith; Lawrence Halprin Associates; Raymond Loewy Associates; Henry Dreyfuss Associates; and dozens of city governments involved in the design of public spaces. He wrote a sociological justification for Bertrand Goldberg's River City development in

Chicago, and, along with Mildred Reed Hall, conducted a ten-year study of Eero Saarinen's John Deere headquarters. Hall also testified on conditions in jails in Washington, DC, was a liaison member of the National Academy of Sciences Building Research Advisory Board, consulted on the Federal Bureau of Standards building specification guidelines, and served on Richard Nixon's task force on quality in federal architecture convened through the National Endowment for the Arts in 1973.

In these capacities—expert witness and professional facilitator—Hall's new science functioned something like a data repository he could draw from to apply to various architectural situations. It was both forward and backward looking, able to explain both the ills of the current environment and their (potential) reform in future structures. These structures were subsequently understood as extensions, the disposition of which was recognized as having certain determinative effects on users. The promise of proxemics was therefore ergonomic—not a mere Tayloristic optimization of bodily zones or an organically shaped physical affordance but rather a kind of ethological and existential ergonomics. Hall's work held out the promise of being able to visualize human "factors" as patterns that might be translated into physical structures. It promised to provide objective guidelines for the manipulation of architecture as sensory apparatus, biological control mechanism, and social palliative. It was as though the perennial dream of the avant-garde—to create a new humanity via design—was finally finding both its scientific justification and a method of implementation.

"In a very deep sense," Hall wrote in 1968, "man is creating different types of people in his slums, his mental hospitals, his cities, and his suburbs."[111] These were people, as far as Hall was concerned, whose bubbles had been forcibly constrained and deformed, whose senses had been artificially overextended. They were social subjects who had been strapped to the Procrustean bed of culture, its institutions, and its physical environment. They were individuals who, as Hall was establishing in his model interview space at IIT—with its cameras clicking, its subjects' eyes meeting and averting, its chairs being pushed around by fractions of inches, and every gesture being coded and computed—were subject to any number of out-of-awareness environmental mechanisms. Architecture in these dynamics was less a container of gestures and users and more of an active agent. It was both a physical and immaterial mechanism shaping and being shaped by its inhabitants. But, more than this, proxemics seemed to be able to trace the degree to which subjectivity—in its racialized, gendered, economic, and existential dimensions—was itself architectural.

Perceptions, thoughts, actions—all were constructed and arranged in specific forms. These forms were patterns that interfaced and co-formed with the external world.

Yet many designers were ambivalent about the architectural promise of proxemics (and environmental design). For what would it mean if some form of universal human data—ergonomic or cultural—could be established? What if proxemic phenomena, psychological comportments, and cultural realities could, in fact, be quantified as architectural standards? Architecture would potentially cease to be a way of producing cultural meaning. This is what Bertrand Goldberg realized as he developed a friendly dialog with Hall after the latter's arrival at IIT. During the months Hall was fine tuning (and expanding) his notation system, he was engaging with Goldberg regarding the nature of human habitation and environmental determination. If optimized human factors were defined, Goldberg feared, what would become of architecture's social function? Writing to Hall, he asked (in the racially charged terms of this moment):

> How does your society change if we don't change it. In other words, can we be arbitrary about making statements on behalf of society or are you going to come up with more scientific information on what the limits are.

> My own worry is that you and Martin Luther King join together in saying that society of a given background cannot live in buildings higher than 8 stories, or 4 stories. You both go further in even saying that this is desirable.

> On the other hand we see another kind of society which is fully equipped to live in buildings perhaps up to 100 stories in height.

> Are these differences to be permanently maintained or what is the process for change? This assumes that change is desirable for reasons that lie even beyond the expressed wishes of a social group. The question is, can the change be made? Obviously all change of whatever nature involves tension, readjustment, and sometimes distress. Doesn't this get into a qualitative judgment about the human condition? And who says tensions are undesirable?[112]

Here—at the moment when public housing was being assessed as racially oppressive and generally inhumane—was an architect asking after humanity itself. Should architecture mold itself to a static, ethno-graphically described subject, or could that subject itself become plastic? What was the determinative interplay between humanity and milieu? Could this dynamic be conceived as a progressive mechanism and not solely an apparatus of deterrence?[113]

"I agree with what you say about the role of the architect," Hall wrote Goldberg several years later in a similar exchange, "not only do I agree but I underscore it. I've always maintained that the job of the scientist was to work on the program or provide data for the program while leaving the design part up to the architect."[114] Hall was no strict determinist, and even though he never relinquished a belief in a biologi-cal or evolutionary basis for human perception and behavior, he was also heavily invested in the idea that people could gain in self-aware-ness and self-actualizing agency. Indeed, one of the political aspects of proxemics was to make cultural systems—bubbles and extensions alike—visible to all so that they might be altered, so that humans could begin to "move through" their environments instead of being "contained within them." This operative impulse was an extension of the basic research Hall was conducting. He propounded a social—frankly utopian—agenda that was in profound sympathy with the perennial modernist dream of individual and social liberation through the cultiva-tion of human sensibility. Architecture and environment provided him a tangible locus where this process of subjection was potentially visible and reformable.

Hall admired Goldberg's Marina City when it was completed in 1964, and about a decade later he would write an essay supporting the magnification of its modernist logic in the form of River City—a project that, though initiated, never reached the megastructural scale Goldberg envisioned. River City was meant to be an integrated urban structure, with all the functions of the city contained in a single building. Acknowledging the radical proposition such a design presented, Hall argued that the world was changing:

The social, political, economic, and technical forms now emerging are so radically different from those of the past they are almost unrecognizable. As a result, the old molds and old solutions no longer work. Because these changes are gradual, and because we are unaccustomed to looking at society as a whole, it is difficult to grasp the fact that man's physical environment—the buildings in which he lives and works—must also change, not just cosmetically, but in design concept.[115]

Here, the metaphor of the mold reverses (or at least muddles) the usual determinist argument. The human here is not a stable entity with recognizable factors to which architecture must conform. Both inhabitants and structures are set in motion, co-forming and co-evolving. In describing this process in this context, Hall was effectively doubling down on the Corbusian conception of the integrated urban tower or structure at a moment when most were abandoning it.

But Hall's rather banal generalizations about molds and extensions were not backed up—even in 1977—by data. And as he continued to seek the architectures of proxemics, the exact dynamics of the movement, or point of contact between, the psychic or social subject continued to prove elusive. IBM Building 701 and his data gathering at CTA stations indicated the presence of potentially tangible proxemic features, but with all too ethereal explanations and principles. These vagaries did not hinder interest in proxemics, however. Perhaps they fueled it. Proxemics came to function in design circles as an objective wedge that could allow architects to broach questions of things like "quality" and "usability" with clients and stakeholders. It offered a way to quantify—in square feet and dollars—human responses to architecture in the forms of creativity, productivity, the release of psychic tensions, and the accommodation of different cultural backgrounds. The incompleteness and vagueness of proxemics aided its multivalence in these situations. It could be mustered for virtually any justification, from the selection of doorknobs to addressing the urban crisis.

In 1971 Edward T. Hall Associates contracted with Skidmore, Owings & Merrill to provide an assessment of the state of the Pruitt-Igoe housing complex in St. Louis. Hall and his wife Mildred traveled to the complex, took notes on its current state, and interviewed residents. Their report took the form of a general essay on considerations for public housing with a list of recommendations for Pruitt-Igoe in particular. It is easy to read these documents and come away with the feeling that the Halls were simply reiterating the well-known problems of the project as design imperatives: "Reduce the monstrous scale of PI" "Create a feeling of community within the project." "Install industrial quality door locks on every apartment, and doors with steel panels." But these modest proposals were couched within a larger vision of holistically designed public housing. They described the necessity of understanding these projects as part of a "total system" of urban life, and, more pointedly, they described public housing as a "social machine" producing, as Hall had suggested earlier, "different types of people." "Basically," their observations read, "we think these projects fail because the tenants have very special needs which are not being met in our society. Housing is just one of these needs."[116]

Perhaps proxemics could have helped designers understand those specific needs. Perhaps not. Regardless, the Halls called for a more integrative approach to public housing that included more purposeful tenant vetting for economic diversity, on-site maintenance crews, schools and childcare, and a well-paid security force recruited from the tenant population (who would design their own uniforms). Recalling Hall's work with the YMCA in Chicago, they also recommended social service programs such as job and interview training. On the architectural side, they put forth propositions such as: "Within the PI community we need to develop an 'urban medieval village,' with housing that offers privacy and security, many small pedestrian walkways, access roads that DO NOT destroy the human scale of our village, facilities for enhancing contact between residents (pubs, both outdoor and indoor restaurants, little shops, paperback libraries, store front social service centers)." These local reforms would then also be connected to infrastructural systems such as "living corridors" that connected the development to the surrounding urban fabric. Remarkably, perhaps, the Halls' imperative that "human constraints should override economic constraints" was met with great enthusiasm. SOM's report was conducted after the vast majority of residents had been moved out and most of the complex had been boarded up. Nonetheless, the firm's "Action Plan"—including the Halls' recommendations—won unanimous approval by the Pruitt-Igoe authority. Walter Netsch sent a triumphant telegram to the Halls declaring that "your isolation will be shattered—shattered for the issues of the urban world." The infamous demolition that then took place in 1972 was actually part of these rehabilitation efforts, which were abandoned shortly after.

The Halls' assessment of Pruitt-Igoe is an early articulation of ideas like those of "defensible space," crime prevention through environmental design (CPTED), "broken windows" policies, and New Urbanism.[117] They anticipated the complex interplay in these models of environmental determinism and human agency. Yet the report sits uneasily between the cynical determinism of the broken window and the (also cynical) community member buy-in of defensible space. Neither approach acknowledged the structural social—racial—inequalities of the spaces they sought to reform and surveil.

While proxemics offered hope for tracking systemic environmental inequality, this was not to be its legacy. By the time his proxemics handbook appeared, in 1974, Hall's science had spun off into technical obscurity and platitudinous justification for arbitrary design decisions.[118]

Take, for instance, these snippets from a normative 1969 design report, *The Office Environment*:

"Ergonomics," "proxemics," "Ekistics"—these are provocative names that describe new theories about human behavior being applied by behavioral scientists, architects and interior designers to studies of the office environment. They represent concepts of relationships between man and man, man and space and man and objects. They are proving to be extremely useful in helping us to understand and meet the psychological and functional needs of the nearly 36 million men and women who spend the majority of daylight hours working in offices.[119]

These new theories, it turned out, revealed some fundamental truisms about effective working environments:

Rooms are pleasingly proportioned—large rooms for the most part with low ceilings that consist of an acoustical material, light in color, and at a single height throughout the office with light fixtures incorporated where necessary. True-white, daylight equivalent lighting is preferred by most.

Natural finishes, like wood, as used on the walls where feasible. Quiet colors with a few bright accents have the greatest appeal. Cool colors, such as blue or green, are used in large areas. Gray has been avoided. [...] Plastic laminate or wood desktops provide a good writing surface.[120]

Here, we essentially have the archetypal image of a 1970s office space, complete with drop ceilings with acoustic panels, fluorescent lighting, wood paneling, garishly painted accent walls, and an overabundance of Formica. Having always assumed that these spaces were the perverse and unconsidered byproduct of purely economic concerns on the part of contractors and business owners, it is shocking to learn that they were actually based on optimal environmental design parameters as prescribed by professional researchers.

But not even these banalities could completely destroy Hall's method, the assimilation of which into the networks of neoliberal capitalism—an assimilation Hall himself eagerly initiated—has continued. While proxemics reappears in anthropological discourse as a historical footnote, or an occasional object of revival, its true legacy is to be found scattered among UX designers looking for objective metrics for human-machine intimacy and pop psychologists promising insight into depoliticized models of "personal space."[121]

Lost in this contemporary uptake of proxemics is precisely its attempt to visualize processes of social determination. Here, personal space was seen not simply as a communicative projection outward from a conscious individual but equally as that field in which social forces were brought to bear on that individual. Interaction in this regard is not something that simply plays out between two or more subjects; rather, it is situated viscerally in an environment comprising subjective and determinative agents, some of which are human, some of which are patterns of behavior that predetermine subjective responses, and some of which are physical objects and architectures.

Historically, then, Hall was one of the first to perceive the "spherological" implications of postindustrialism.[122] He was one of the first to identify new forms of humanity being produced on station platforms and in offices, living rooms, city squares, and housing projects during this period of social pressure and atomization. As these processes came into view, it became apparent that architecture and environment were not neutral backdrops for social interaction. They were active agents whose material and aesthetic structures extended and circumscribed the perceptual, cognitive, and bodily potentiality of the subject. Wielded by social scientists or designers, proxemics, with its dual understanding of humanity as both territorially constrained and technologically extended, offered a model for not only reshaping existing environments but making users aware of the socially, psychologically, and existentially determinative mechanisms of their surroundings. The most sympathetic reading would understand it as potentially a method of making both deterrence and agency visible as interactional environmental patterns.

THE PROXEMICS ARCHIVE

This book is not an attempt to rebuke or correct the legacy and contemporary uses of proxemics. Nor is it a call to recuperate a proxemically sensitive understanding of human interaction. It is, rather, a first step in historicizing an apparatus for the visualization and instrumentalization of human data and difference. Not unique in kind, but certainly in intensity and exposure, proxemics may be one of the most tangible ways we have to trace the movement of knowledge from the social sciences to the design disciplines. It also differs from other measuring instruments by its plainly aesthetic foundations. It was a science that did not rely on direct observation because its objects did not exist in isolation. They only existed as fleeting arcs traced by human movement, lines of sight, and the pushing and pulling of things in the environment, as the architecture of perceptual limits themselves.

These ambiguities highlight the surprise of finding such rich visual materials in Hall's archive, all of which speak to the difficulty of making tangible these ethereal existential phenomena. How might it be possible to graph the infinite nuance of human interaction? To diagram the conditioning mechanisms of the environment? To trace the virtual lines of force that emerge from a background only to be integrated into the psyche of the social subject? How could a grainy snapshot capture all of these things? The obvious failure of these techniques of observation and documentation should not divert us from a meditation on what they actually did record: not a scientifically defined object but a way of seeing, an aesthetics of social knowledge. In this sense, the object being historicized here is neither a specific anthropological method nor a series of architectural projects. It is, rather, a way of looking—a "period eye" attuned to particular political and environmental realities.

That period eye becomes apparent not only in the content of the textual and visual documents in the archive but also in their materials and forms. The distinctive blur of the mimeographed letter; the frayed edges of perforated dot matrix paper sheets folded into thick, impenetrable stacks; the distinctive linework and caricatures of period comic strips that one knows are sexist before even reading the captions; and the slot boxes filled with pinkening slides all tell the tale of an infinite universe of data being opened up and collated at the precise moment that analog techniques were giving way to digital ones. The examples also speak to a growing sense of futility in tracking that data, the feeling of being overwhelmed by its amount and underwhelmed by the anemic output of new and old assessment tools. Collectively, somehow, the ensemble of heterogenous materials conveys a great deal of affect. The quantitative ambitions of the early 1960s give way to the resigned qualitative tone of the documents a decade later.

One might expect the photographs in the collection to convey these shifting sentiments most poignantly. But, as with photographs in general, they occlude more than they reveal. They could never serve as proof for Hall's observations. He always needed to be present (in person or text) to point out their salient details. Nor could they ever function individually. They always required a companion piece (or several) whose similarities and differences could be observed. While most images were used as raw material for coding, Hall would take other photos pasted onto cardstock to meetings to show clients as examples of proxemic and territorial phenomena. These often juxtaposed images of animals and humans in surprisingly analogical situations—crowding together or unconsciously respecting the invisible boundaries of territory. Similar slides were made for public lectures. Others were prepared for publication. Subjects have numbers above their heads, or lines and dashes drawn around their bodies. Some images are line drawings traced from photographs. Most photographs, however, never saw the light of day. Hall filed them away, their images transposed in his memory, perhaps, as thousands of bubbles pushing and pulling subjects through the cities he visited.

The ambiguity in what these images should do vis-à-vis proxemics parallels Hall's compulsive and self-reflexive engagement with the medium of photography itself. This included his intimate knowledge of the ways in which anthropology and photography had co-formed in the twentieth century, added to a keen awareness of the tenuousness of any attempt to record objective observations. These images were produced as photography's claims to truth were being questioned in some quarters and upheld as an article of faith in others. Hall's understanding of the medium hovered between a strictly evidentiary conception and a postmodern view of the photographic image as a highly mediated apparatus. We might therefore understand these documents as part of a genealogy of contemporaneous philosophical meditations on photography, film, and images more generally from Stanley Cavell's *The World Viewed* (1971) to John Berger's *Ways of Seeing* (1972).[123] Hall's evolving understanding of the proxemics of observation, photographing, and analysis (on the part of both informants and researchers) also recalls the famous work that initiated the project of cinema verité: Edgar Morin and Jean Rouch's *Chronique d'un été* of 1960. The images of crowds and people interacting might also bring to mind Francis Ford Coppola's classic 1974 meditation on paranoia in the surveillance society, *The Conversation*. Certainly unwittingly, Coppola's grainy, telescopic shots of individuals meeting in crowded plazas for surreptitious exchanges were duplicated in William H. Whyte's book and film *The Social Life of Small Urban Spaces* (1980).[124] Unsurprisingly, Whyte cited Hall's work as a primary influence.

Hall seemed to pack all the ambivalence of these heterogenous sources into a single scientific and photographic practice. He understood the photograph as both a tool for, and an object of, analysis. Even as he was snapping thousands of pictures, he could never shake the feeling that their form and content, *pace* Bourdieu, were being socially predetermined. The camera, after all, was one of the most significant human extensions. Hall's self-reflexivity in this regard produced a profound irony. The more he attempted to remove himself from the processes of making and analyzing photographs—via

high-speed shutters, tracings, or an immersive viewing apparatus—
the more ambiguous and arbitrary those images became, the more he
himself was required as their mediator and interpreter. Perhaps this
is one reason why the archive seems to be structured around an empty
center. All the evidence points not directly to but *toward* something
that always eludes identification, toward a conception of the human
that is never able to emerge.

The proxemics archive, in other words, is no *Family of Man*. It seems
to be neither a quest for universality nor a celebration of difference.[125]
While Hall ostensibly set out to record instances of cultural contrasts in
the use of space, the distinctness of those behavioral patterns is lost
in their infinite cross-referencing and transposition. Where Hall claimed
to be able to identify cultural difference by looking at crowds or pictures
of crowds, contemporary viewers might find themselves desperately
seeking evidence in the surroundings—like the style of the architecture
or the language on the signs—to identify the locations and contexts of
the human subjects. Collectively, then, Hall's archive rests uneasily—
and happens to occupy a chronological midpoint—between the human-
ist aspirations of Edward Steichen and the ideological self-awareness
of the compendium created by Larry Sultan and Mike Mandel in their
seminal conceptual experiment *Evidence*, from 1977. In that work,
decontextualized photographs of human bodies and technical apparatuses interact within and across dozens of scenes of scientific and
military initiatives whose original purpose is not only lost to time but
further obscured by the photographic documents themselves.

But perhaps these historical and perceptual vicissitudes—the way
in which an accumulation of evidence seems rather to undermine than
to reinforce a particular endeavor—are common to all visual archives.
This seems to be the case with the obvious precedents: the collections
of photographic images of classical and postclassical art amassed by
Aby Warburg, or André Malraux's *musée imaginaire*. In both of these
projects, it was the movement between images as much as the images
themselves that carried significance. And what that significance was,
exactly, is obscure for contemporary viewers. But unlike Gerhard
Richter's *Atlas*, for instance, compiled during the same years as Hall's
project, the proxemics archive was never meant to be seen in its
entirety. Further, Hall's compendium was not generated from a seemingly detached eye scanning a world full of ready-made images. He
lacked Richter's blasé curatorial attitude.

No, Hall was looking for something, something that only appeared
in the anamorphic spaces between people and their worlds, spaces
that could never entirely be sutured together. He paranoically attempted

to photograph these spaces, to find them in media images and illustrations. And though he was unconcerned with anything like a photographic medium specificity, his compulsive attempts to photograph out-of-awareness social structures on the surfaces of bodies and environmental structures affect us as a constant collapsing of Barthes's categories of the *studium* and *punctum* into one another, the manifest always falling away and penetrating the latent as the latter advances. Accordingly, we should not seek here a content or subject matter in the usual sense. Even the most facile observation—that these are visual representations of people in certain situations—is not entirely accurate. For these are not so much pictures of bodies or subjects as of environmental forces impinging upon them. They are pictures of and notations for interstices, for the patterns and frames—what Hall would have described as "culture"—that are always supporting, constraining, encircling, and effecting us. They are images of backgrounds and intergrounds, not of figures. They are yardsticks for social distance. They are the silhouettes of alienation.

Hall's devotion to a literal model of perceiving these phantasmatic forms is apparent in the materials presented here. That belief (no matter how vulgar its empiricism) was itself enabled by new regimes of visualization and computation.[126] For the first time it seemed possible to back up far enough from social phenomena to quantify and aggregate their preconditions, to map the largest and most nebulous structures and their passage to the psyche of the subject. But the shift in scales such a project implies, the necessity of identifying a common substance for the most disparate objects, the attempt to discern human backgrounds as though they were figures, to perceive the social limitations of perception itself—these demands would prove too much for Hall's nascent science. They render his data gathering not only insufficient, but misguided. In this regard, the batches of photos, coding charts, drawings of different types of sensory space, and computer printouts are an accumulation without resolution. They are a series of false starts. A visual catalog of individuals standing in for social structures. Hundreds upon hundreds of crystallizations of interactional moments. Emergent situations arrested in historical time. The writing of infinite lines so that they might be read between.

1   Edward T. Hall, *The Hidden Dimension* (1966; reprint, New York: Anchor, 1990), 4. Emphasis in original.

2   Edward T. Hall, *Beyond Culture* (New York: Anchor, 1976).

3   Georges Canguilhem, "The Living and Its Milieu," in *Knowledge of Life*, trans. Stefanos Geroulanos and Daniela Ginsburg (1965; reprint, New York: Fordham University Press, 2008). See also Jakob von Uexküll, *A Foray into the Worlds of Animals and Humans*, trans. Joseph D. O'Neil (1934; reprint, Minneapolis: University of Minnesota Press, 2010).

4   Peter L. Berger and Thomas Luckmann, *The Social Construction of Reality: A Treatise in the Sociology of Knowledge* (New York: Penguin, 1966); Marshall McLuhan, *Understanding Media: The Extensions of Man* (New York: McGraw-Hill, 1964); Thomas Kuhn, *The Structure of Scientific Revolutions* (Chicago: University of Chicago Press, 1962). These postwar statements can be linked to a longer lineage of linguistic constructionism including Wittgenstein and Edward Sapir. See Ludwig Wittgenstein, *Tractatus Logico-philosophicus* (London: Keegan Paul, Trench, Trubner, 1922), and Edward Sapir, *Language: An Introduction to the Study of Speech* (New York: Harcourt Brace, 1921).

5   Here I refer to the mutations in social philosophy engendered in the French context by a rereading of the works of Marx, Freud, and Nietzsche through the lens of the linguistic structuralism of Ferdinand de Saussure.

6   Berger and Luckmann, *The Social Construction of Reality*, 67.

7   Hall used the formulation of "high-" and "low-context" cultures throughout his work beginning in *The Silent Language*. Within the anthropological subfield of intercultural communications, these categories would prove more enduring than proxemics itself. Edward T. Hall, *The Silent Language* (1959; reprint, New York: Anchor Books, 1973).

8   Proxemics still freely floats through sociology, anthropology, psychology, and subdisciplines such as social neuroscience, psychophysics, cognitive ethology, and affective science. In most of these contexts, it functions as a decontextualized shorthand for nonverbal bodily responses and communication. With varying degrees of historical awareness, contemporary researchers seem always to be rediscovering both the possibilities and pitfalls of attempting to record and interpret postures, lines of sight, social distance, and so on in "real time" and in "natural contexts." See J. A. Harrigan, "Proxemics, Kinesics, and Gaze," in *Series in Affective Science: The New Handbook of Methods in Nonverbal Behavior Research*, ed. J. A. Harrigan, R. Rosenthal, and K. R. Scherer (Oxford: Oxford University Press, 2005), 137–198, and Cade McCall and Tania Singer, "Facing Off with Unfair Others: Introducing Proxemic Imaging as an Implicit Measure of Approach and Avoidance during Social Interaction," *PLoS ONE* 10, no. 2 (February 2015), https://doi.org/10.1371/journal.pone.0117532.

9   The selection represents a fraction of the archive, from the Papers of Edward Twitchell Hall, 1930–1979, University of Arizona Libraries, Special Collections (hereafter abbreviated ETH Papers).

10   Edward T. Hall, *An Anthropology of Everyday Life: An Autobiography* (New York: Doubleday, 1992), 189.

11   Retrospectively, Hall acknowledged an analogous convergence of tangible and social patterning. Recalling his experience in New Mexico, he wrote: "The Hopi religious world is a whole; it is tangible, manifest, and very real to them. When I was there, its palpable presence covered and enclosed each village like a giant invisible dome. In many ways the Hopi village was like a cathedral—the architecture was invisible, but it was there, and it was sacred." Hall, *An Anthropology of Everyday Life*, 113. Hall saw culture as constituting an invisible architecture for all people, a structuring of environment and perception—the extending and constraining "invisible domes" of the social subject—whose structures he sought to trace.

12   Ruth Benedict, *Patterns of Culture* (New York: Houghton Mifflin, 1934).

13   See Marisa G. S. Peirano, "When Anthropology Is at Home: The Different Contexts of a Single Discipline," *Annual Review of Anthropology* 27 (1998): 105–128.

14   Fred Turner, *The Democratic Surround: Multimedia and American Liberalism from World War II to the Psychedelic Sixties* (Chicago: University of Chicago Press, 2013).

15   Margaret Mead, *And Keep Your Powder Dry: An Anthropologist Looks at America* (New York: Morrow, 1965).

16   Edward T. Hall, "Proxemics," *Current Anthropology* 9, no. 2/3 (April–June 1968): 83–108. In the comments, old friend Ray Birdwhistell complained that Hall needed to "straighten out the epistemology" in his generalizations, as his various appropriations from biology, psychology, anthropology, and linguistics were incompatible. Others echoed these sentiments, complaining that the categories of nature and nurture were hopelessly confused within Hall's model, which moved from territoriality to communication. Others complained that the image of the bubble was simplistic. Some recognized the potential for cultural or racist reductivism. Frank Lynch opined that he would like to see "fewer undifferentiated 'Americans,' 'Arabs,' and 'Greeks.'" Hall's one-time coauthor George L. Trager even expressed his dissatisfaction with the term "proxemics."

17   Hall, *The Hidden Dimension*, 172–173.

18   On nonverbal and intercultural communication, as well as Hall's other analytical frameworks such as "high-" and "low-context" communication, "contact" and "non-contact" cultures, "situational frames," and so on, see Dar Gillespie and Ann Leffler, "Theories of Nonverbal Behavior: A Critical Review of Proxemics Research," *Sociological Theory* 1 (1983): 102–154; Frederick Erickson, "Origins: A Brief Intellectual and Technological History of the Emergence of Multimodal Discourse Analysis," in *Discourse and Technology: Multimodal Discourse Analysis*, ed. Philip Le Vine and Ron Scollon (Washington, DC: Georgetown University Press, 2004), 196–207; and Carol Zinner Dophin, "Beyond Hall: Variables in the Use of Personal Space in Intercultural Transactions," *Howard Journal of Communications* 1, no. 1 (Spring 1988): 23–28.

19   For more on the development of intercultural communications studies at the Department of State, see Wendy Leeds-Hurwitz, "Notes on the History of Intercultural Communication: The Foreign Service Institute and the Mandate for Intercultural Training," *Quarterly Journal of Speech* 76 (1990): 262–281.

20   Jennifer S. Light, *From Warfare to Welfare: Defense Intellectuals and Urban Problems in Postwar America* (Baltimore: Johns Hopkins University Press, 2003).

21   David H. Price, *Cold War Anthropology: The CIA, the Pentagon, and the Growth of Dual Use Anthropology* (Durham, NC: Duke University Press, 2016), 369–388.

22   Human Ecology Fund, "Research Grants in Human Ecology," unpublished document, ETH Papers, box 1, folder 1.

23   Price observes that the book was positively reviewed in *Studies in Intelligence* in 1959. Price, *Cold War Anthropology*, 522 n20.

24   Hall, *The Silent Language*, 187, 129.

25   Chris Oliver, "The Absence of Edward T. Hall in American Anthropology," *Multicultural Relations* 6 (2009): 1–19; Sally O. Hastings, George W. Musambira, and Rana Ayoub, "Revisiting Edward T. Hall's Work on Arabs and Olfaction with Implications for Intercultural Communication Scholarship," *Journal for Intercultural Communications Research* 40, no. 1 (2011): 3–20.

26   Edmund Leach, "Nonsense and Sensibility," *New York Review of Books* 10, no. 10 (May 23, 1968).

27   Hall, *An Anthropology of Everyday Life*, 150–153.

28   Berger and Luckmann, *The Social Construction of Reality*, 75, 77.

29   Hall, *The Silent Language*, 111. Emphasis in original.

30   Georg Simmel, *The Sociology of Georg Simmel*, trans. Kurt H. Wolff (Glencoe, IL: Free Press, 1950), 379–395.

31   Simmel, *The Sociology of Georg Simmel*, 418–419.

32   Berger and Luckmann, *The Social Construction of Reality*, 203.

33   In nonverbal communications studies, Thomas Bruneau introduced the term "chronemics" with explicit reference to Hall: "It is time, not space, which is truly the 'hidden dimension' or variable in the study of human communication." Thomas Bruneau, "Chronemics: The Study of Time in Human Interaction," *Communication* 6, no. 2 (July 1977): 1. Despite this jab, Hall had conceptualized the notions of monochronic and polychronic time as facets of cultural communication as early as 1959. See also Edward T. Hall, *The Dance of Life: The Other Dimension of Time* (New York: Doubleday, 1983).

34   Michel Foucault, "Of Other Spaces," in *Architecture Culture 1943–1968: A Documentary Anthology*, ed. Joan Ockman and Edward Eigen (New York: Columbia University Graduate School of Architecture, Planning, and Preservation; Rizzoli, 1993), 420–426.

35   Henri Lefebvre, *The Production of Space*, trans. Donald Nicholson-Smith (1974;

reprint, Oxford: Blackwell, 1991). Like Hall, Lefebvre would turn his attention to time in his later work: Henri Lefebvre, *Elements of Rhythmanalysis*, trans. Stuart Elden (1992; reprint, London: Continuum, 2004).

36   On the concept of social space, see Jeanne Haffner, *The View from Above: The Science of Social Space* (Cambridge, MA: MIT Press, 2013).

37   Roland Barthes, *How to Live Together: Novelistic Simulations of Some Everyday Spaces*, trans. Kate Briggs (1976; reprint, New York: Columbia University Press, 2013), 112.

38   Pierre Bourdieu, "Social Space and Symbolic Power," *Sociological Theory* 7, no. 1 (Spring 1989): 18; Bourdieu, *Distinction: A Social Critique of the Judgment of Taste*, trans. Richard Nice (1979; reprint, Cambridge, MA: Harvard University Press, 1984).

39   Hall, "Proxemics," 87.

40   Pierre Bourdieu, *Photography: A Middle-Brow Art*, trans. Shaun Whiteside (1965; reprint, Stanford, CA: Stanford University Press, 1990), 5.

41   Hall, *The Silent Language*, 187.

42   The first publication to describe proxemics was Edward T. Hall, "Proxemics: The Study of Man's Spatial Relations and Boundaries," in *Man's Image in Medicine and Anthropology*, ed. Iago Galdston (Madison, WI: International University Press, 1963). An unpublished draft from 1961, titled "Spatial Relations and Man's Physiology and Psychology," is in ETH Papers. This was followed by Edward T. Hall, "A System for the Notation of Proxemic Behavior," *American Anthropologist* 65, no. 5 (October 1963): 1003–1026. Hall then published *The Hidden Dimension* (1966), which was about the cultural implications of proxemics but did little to advance it methodologically. Finally, a more or less complete notation system, designed for computer processing, was published as Edward T. Hall, *Handbook for Proxemic Research* (Washington, DC: Society for the Anthropology of Visual Communication, 1974).

43   Hall, "Notation of Proxemic Behavior," 1003.

44   Hall, *The Hidden Dimension*, 1.

45   Hall, "Notation of Proxemic Behavior," 1022.

46   Edward T. Hall, "The Language of Space," *Landscape* 10 (Autumn 1960): 41–44.

47   Hall, "Notation of Proxemic Behavior," 1003–1026; Edward T. Hall, "Quality in Architecture—an Anthropological View," *Journal of the American Institute of Architects* 40, no.1 (July 1963): 44–48. The latter was presented at the AIA conference in Miami that year.

48   Maurice Grosser, *The Painter's Eye* (New York: Rinehart, 1951); Alexander Dorner, *The Way Beyond Art* (1947; reprint, New York: New York University Press, 1958); Ernö Goldfinger, "The Sensation of Space," *Architectural Review* 90 (November 1941): 128–131; Goldfinger, "Urbanism and Spatial Order," *Architectural Review* 90 (December 1941), 163–166; Goldfinger, "The Elements of Enclosed Space," *Architectural Review* 91 (January 1942), 5–8.

49   Kevin Lynch, *The Image of the City* (Cambridge MA: MIT Press, 1960). Hall wrote to Lynch at this time, praising his "ingeneous [*sic*] system that [he] had developed for getting people to note down what they had seen as they traveled a standard route." Hall to Kevin Lynch, November 7, 1961, ETH Papers, uncataloged materials.

50   Hall, "Notation of Proxemic Behavior," 1006–1007.

51   John Harwood, "The Interface: Ergonomics and the Aesthetics of Survival," in *Governing by Design: Architecture, Economy, and Politics in the Twentieth Century*, ed. Aggregate (Pittsburgh: University of Pittsburgh Press, 2012), 83.

52   See Jay Ruby, *Picturing Culture: Explorations of Film and Anthropology* (Chicago: University of Chicago Press, 2000), 62; Lee D. Baker, *Anthropology and the Racial Politics of Culture* (Durham, NC: Duke University Press, 2010), 211. On the ways such studies actually shaped initial understandings of media, see Brian Hochman, *Savage Preservation: The Ethnographic Origins of Modern Media Technology* (Minneapolis: University of Minnesota Press, 2014).

53   Kinesics and proxemics were followed by Alan Lomax's Choreometrics. On the relation among these systems, see Brenda Farnell, "Birdwhistell, Hall, Lomax and the Origins of Visual Anthropology," *Visual Anthropology* 16, no. 1 (2003): 43–55.

54   Birdwhistell and Bateson participated in Frieda Fromm-Reichmann's seminar at Stanford's new Center for Advanced Study in the Behavioral Sciences (CASBS) in 1955–56. They contributed to a multidisciplinary

analysis of family communication, later compiled in Norman McQuown, ed., "The Natural History of an Interview" (1971), unpublished MS, University of Chicago Library Microfilm Collection of Manuscripts on Cultural Anthropology. One of the other participants in that study, George Trager, had also worked with Hall. See Edward T. Hall and George L. Trager, *The Analysis of Culture* (Washington, DC: Foreign Service Institute, 1953).

55 Ray Birdwhistell, *Kinesics and Context: Essays on Body Motion Communication* (Philadelphia: University of Pennsylvania Press, 1970), 3.

56 Even now, in psychological and anthropological nonverbal communications studies, the desideratum of a comprehensive "alphabet" of human gesture dangles elusively. See Conrad Izquierdo, and M. Teresa Anguera, "Movement Notation Revisited: Syntax of the Common Morphokinetic Alphabet (CMA) System," *Frontiers in Psychology* 9 (August 2018), https://www.ncbi.nlm.nih.gov/pmc/articles/PMC6110945.

57 Seth Barry Water, "Scrutinizing: Film and Microanalysis of Behavior," *Grey Room* 66 (Winter 2017): 32–69.

58 Phillip Thiel, "A Sequence-Experience Notation for Architectural and Urban Spaces," *Town Planning Review* 32, no. 1 (April 1961): 33–52.

59 Lawrence Halprin, "Fort Worth City Walk Map" (1974), reprinted in Alison Hirsch, "Scoring the Participatory City: Lawrence (& Anna) Halprin's Take Part Process," *Journal of Architectural Education* 64, no. 2 (March 2011): 127–140.

60 Robert Sommer, *Personal Space: The Behavioral Basis of Design* (Englewood Cliffs, NJ: Prentice Hall, 1969).

61 Hall, *The Hidden Dimension*, 65.

62 Hall, *The Silent Language*, 113.

63 Hall, *The Silent Language*, 79.

64 For more on the general content and tenor of this correspondence, see Everett M. Rogers, "The Extensions of Men: The Correspondence of Marshall McLuhan and Edward T. Hall," *Mass Communication and Society* 3, no. 1 (2000): 117–135.

65 For an excellent account of McLuhan's other sources for the term, see Richard Cavell, *McLuhan in Space: A Cultural Geography* (Toronto: University of Toronto Press, 2002), 256–257 n52.

66 Marshall McLuhan to Hall, September 16, 1964, ETH Papers, box 8, folder 28. McLuhan would repeat that claim to Fuller the same year: "If one says that any new technology creates a new environment, that is better than saying the medium is the message." Marshall McLuhan to Buckminster Fuller, September 17, 1964, in *Letters of Marshall McLuhan*, ed. Matie Molinaro, Corinne McLuhan, and William Toye (Oxford: Oxford University Press, 1987), 308–309.

67 Buckminster Fuller, *Nine Chains to the Moon* (Philadelphia: J. B. Lippincott, 1938), 68.

68 Marshall McLuhan, *Understanding Media: The Extensions of Man* (New York: McGraw-Hill, 1964).

69 Edward T. Hall, *Beyond Culture* (New York: Anchor, 1976), 25.

70 Hall, *Beyond Culture*, 25–40.

71 Hall to Marshall McLuhan, March 9, 1962, ETH Papers, box 8, folder 27.

72 John J. Christian, Vagn Flyger, and David E. Davis, "Factors in the Mass Mortality of a Herd of Sika Deer, *Cervus nippon*," *Chesapeake Science* 1, no. 2 (June 1960): 79–95; John B. Calhoun, "Population Density and Social Pathology," *Scientific American* 206, no. 2 (1962): 139–148.

73 Calhoun quoted in Hall, *The Hidden Dimension*, 26.

74 Tom Wolfe, "O Rotten Gotham—Sliding Down into the Behavioral Sink" (1966), reprinted in *The Pump House Gang* (New York: Bantam, 1968), 233. "If I remember that day," Wolfe recalled, "we first went to Grand Central. We did all that, went down in the subways, walked around in the middle of Manhattan a bit; then *New York* magazine hired a car. We got in the car. There was a driver so we could both talk and look at things, and we went all through Harlem and all over the place." "'Tom Wolfe' by David Bellamy," in *Conversations with Tom Wolfe*, ed. Dorothy Scura (Jackson: University Press of Mississippi, 1990), 54.

75 Wolfe, "O Rotten Gotham," 233–234. For more on the popular reception of "the sink," see Edmund Ramsden and John Adams, "Escaping the Laboratory: The Rodent Experiments of John B. Calhoun and Their Cultural Influence," *Journal of Social History* 42, no. 3 (Spring 2009): 761–797.

76 Hall, *The Hidden Dimension*, 111–112.

77 These observations on German and Arab culture can be found in Hall, *The Hidden Dimension*, 126 and 144, respectively.

78   Hans O. Mauksch to Hall, December 28, 1962, ETH Papers, box 7, folder 11.

79   Edward T. Hall, "Ethnic Use of Micro-Space in Interethnic Encounters," Final Report MH08045 (undated), ETH Papers, box 1, folder 1.

80   According to an untitled press release (January 18, 1966), ETH Papers, box 7, folder 11: "In the IIT Center for Proxemics Research, Hall has been concentrating on studying ethnic groups which form the US urban population, and plans to develop cooperative research with the IIT Institute of Design and the university's architecture department so that both products and buildings can be made more satisfactory for their users."

81   The account given here of these experiments is greatly simplified. Hall's own account in the *Handbook for Proxemic Research* details exact procedures, changes in method, and other evolutions of his system.

82   Sarah Lewis, "The Racial Bias Built into Photography," *New York Times*, April 25, 2019.

83   Hall, *Handbook for Proxemic Research*, 8.

84   Hall, *Handbook for Proxemic Research*, 42.

85   Hall to Marshall McLuhan, February 8, 1971, ETH Papers, uncataloged materials.

86   Hall, *Handbook for Proxemic Research*, 2–15.

87   Hall, *Handbook for Proxemic Research*, 32.

88   Gregory Bateson and Margaret Mead, *Balinese Character: A Photographic Analysis* (New York: Academy of Sciences, 1942); Paul Byers, "Still Photography in the Systematic Recording and Analysis of Behavioral Data," *Human Organization* 23, no. 1 (Spring 1964), 78–84; John Collier Jr., *Visual Anthropology: Photography as a Research Method* (New York: Holt, Rhinehart and Winston, 1967).

89   For Collier, photographs could be used in addition to verbal communication when interviewing research informants. A photograph, usually from the subject's community, might be able to elicit different responses than merely asking a question. Collier, *Visual Anthropology*, 99–115.

90   See Douglas Harper, "Talking about Pictures: A Case for Photo Elicitation," *Visual Studies* 17, no. 1 (2002): 13–26.

91   "We came to understand the image history of objectivity as an account of kinds of sight. Atlases had implications for who the scientist aspired to be, for how knowledge was most securely acquired, and for what kinds of things there were in the world. To embrace objectivity—or one of its alternatives—was not only to practice a science but also to pattern a self." Lorraine Daston and Peter Galison, *Objectivity* (New York: Zone, 2007), 10.

92   Hall, *Handbook for Proxemic Research,* 12.

93   On the notion of sensory deprivation in impoverished neighborhoods, see Mical Raz, *What's Wrong with the Poor: Psychiatry, Race, and the War on Poverty* (Chapel Hill: University of North Carolina Press, 2013), 142–168.

94   Hall, *The Hidden Dimension*, 129.

95   Alex Anthony Baker, Richard Llewlyn Davies, and Paul Sivadon, *Psychiatric Services and Architecture* (Geneva: World Health Organization, 1960).

96   Edward T. Hall, "The Language of Space," *Landscape* 10 (1960): 41–44; Hall, "The Madding Crowd Space and Its Organization as a Factor in Mental Health," *Landscape* 12 (1962): 26–30.

97   Goldfinger, "The Sensation of Space," 128–131; Goldfinger, "Urbanism and Spatial Order," 163–166; Goldfinger, "The Elements of Enclosed Space," 5–8.

98   Hall to Ernö Goldfinger, February 21, 1963, ETH Papers, box 5, folder 22.

99   "Alexander and his group studied the transit systems of New York, Chicago, Philadelphia and Toronto; talked with a cross section of those involved in transit, from administrators to janitors to passengers; consulted a number of behavioral scientists; and fed their findings through computers." "BART: The Bay Area Takes a Billion Dollar Ride," *Architectural Forum* 124, no. 6 (June 1966): 49.

100   Don Emmons to Hall, February 7, 1964, ETH Papers, uncataloged materials.

101   Christopher Alexander to Hall, January 27, 1964, ETH Papers, uncataloged materials.

102   Edward T. Hall, untitled report, 1964, ETH Papers, uncataloged materials.

103   "The atoms of environmental structure are *relations*. Relations are geometrical patterns. They are the simplest geometrical patterns in a building which can be functionally right or wrong. A list of the relations required in a building replaces the design program, and the first stages of sketch design." Christopher Alexander and Barry Poyner, *The Atoms of Environmental Structure*

(working paper, no. 2, Center for Planning and Development Research, the Institute of Urban and Regional Development, University of California, Berkeley, 1966), 1.

104 Hoffman was a coauthor of a 1957 memo that set out basic considerations for spatial arrangement of this increasingly common building type. The memo covered many topics, with special emphasis on "communication": "the transfer of information, material, and persons from one point to another." Laboratory Planning Committee, "First Report of Laboratory Planning Committee," unpublished memo (September 6, 1957), US Bureau of Standards, Washington, DC.

105 Hall to Norton S. Brown, November 22, 1961, ETH Papers, uncataloged material.

106 Kenny Cupers, "Laboratory Modules and the Subjectivity of the Knowledge Worker," in *Use Matters: An Alternative History of Architecture*, ed. Kenny Cupers (London: Routledge, 2013), 51–68.

107 This type of interface would become IBM's primary concern during these very same years: John Harwood, *The Interface: IBM and the Transformation of Corporate Design* (Minneapolis: University of Minnesota Press, 2011).

108 Mary Louise Lobsinger, "Two Cambridges: Models, Methods, Systems, and Expertise," in *A Second Modernism: MIT, Architecture, and the 'Techno-Social' Moment*, ed. Arindam Dutta (Cambridge, MA: MIT School of Architecture and Planning; MIT Press, 2013), 652–685.

109 In 1966 George McCue updated its curriculum with modules including "Environmental Control Systems" and "History of the Environment." Robert Berdahl, foreword to Waverly Lowell, Elizabeth Byrne, and Betsy Frederick-Rothwell, *Design on the Edge: A Century of Teaching Architecture at the University of California, Berkeley, 1903–2003* (Berkeley: College of Environmental Design, University of California, Berkeley, 2009), 22.

110 Off campus, Donald Appleyard and Kenneth Craik established the Environmental Simulation Laboratory in 1973. Anthony Raynsford, "Simulating Spatial Experience i n the People's Berkeley: The Urban Design Experiments of Donald Appleyard and Kenneth Craik," *Design and Culture* 6, no. 1 (2014): 45–64.

111 Hall, "Proxemics" (1968), 85.

112 Bertrand Goldberg to Hall, November 21, 1966, ETH Papers, uncataloged materials.

113 Goldberg expressed a similar ambivalence after the Halls began joining Doxiadis's Delos cruises: "My complaint with Doxiadis is that he wishes to correct the traffic patterns of the automobile rather than eliminate them. It is a matter for technology to improve the mechanics of our transportation rather than for the planner to accommodate the improprieties of our system." Bertrand Goldberg to Hall, November 21, 1966, ETH Papers, uncataloged materials.

114 Hall to Bertrand Goldberg, November 25, 1969, ETH Papers, uncataloged material.

115 Edward T. Hall Associates, "River City: Vertical Villages of Future" (July 1977), ETH Papers, uncataloged material.

116 Edward T. Hall and Mildred Reed Hall, "Memo to Pruitt Igoe Action Team" (November 15, 1971), ETH Papers, Box 13, Folder 25.

117 Joy Knoblauch, "Defensible Space and the Open Society," *Aggregate* 2 (March 2015), http://we-aggregate.org/piece/defensible-space-and-the-open-society. On broken windows and biopolitics, see Reinhold Martin, *The Urban Apparatus: Mediapolitics and the City* (Minneapolis: University of Minnesota Press, 2018).

118 For an example of this technical obscurity, see O. Michael Watson, "Conflicts and Directions in Proxemic Research," *Journal of Communication* 22, no. 4 (December 1972): 443–459.

119 Lawrence Wheeler, *The Office Environment* (Chicago: ISD Inc., 1969), 5. "ISD was founded as Interior Space Design in 1960 as a subsidiary of Perkins & Will with offices in Chicago and New York." Monica Geran, "ISD; A Three-Part Report," *Interior Design*, October 1, 1984. The firm commissioned this study from Ewing Miller Associates, an Indiana architecture firm notable for its early adoption of behavioral research methods. Ewing H. Miller II partnered with Dr. Lawrence Wheeler to form ISD's own Behavioral Research Department. For more on Ewing Miller, see Michael Flowers, "Behavior and Design: The Architecture of Ewing H. Miller II" (master's thesis, Ball State University, 2015), https://cardinalscholar.bsu.edu/bitstream/handle/123456789/199562/FlowersM_2015-2_BODY.pdf.

120   Wheeler, *The Office Environment*, 7.
121   This process of assimilation was already evident, for instance, in the work of Robert Sommer. Hall knew Sommer through his old acquaintance the psychiatrist Humphrey Osmund, for whom Sommer had worked as research assistant. See Sommer, *Personal Space*.
122   Peter Sloterdijk, *Foams: Spheres III*, trans. Wieland Hoban (South Pasadena, CA: Semiotext(e), 2016).
123   Stanley Cavell, *The World Viewed: Reflections on the Ontology of Film* (Cambridge, MA: Harvard University Press, 1971); John Berger, *Ways of Seeing* (London: Penguin, 1972).
124   William H. Whyte, *The Social Life of Small Urban Spaces* (Washington, DC: Conservation Foundation, 1980).
125   For a recent analysis of these different interpretations of *The Family of Man*, see Ariella Azoulay, "'The Family of Man': A Visual Universal Declaration of Human Rights," in *The Human Snapshot*, ed. Thomas Keenan and Tirdad Zolghadr (Berlin: Sternberg, 2013), 19–48.
126   Orit Halpern, *Beautiful Data: A History of Vision and Reason since 1945* (Durham, NC: Duke University Press, 2015).

Note on the Images

The selection of the images here betrays the art historian's proclivity toward tangibility and the architecture historian's demand for situatedness. Additionally, the presentation is fundamentally incomplete. Most of the series present tiny samples of much larger bodies of images. This is especially true of Series 3, which presents prints from Hall's early 1960s activity with his Minox. Much of the material itself is incomplete. Series 11–12 are drawn from uncataloged material in the archive and may never find definitive attribution. Materials are grouped by both chronology and theme, charting the ebbs and flows of Hall's efforts at quantification and his indulgence in touristic impressionism. If subjects and images seem scattered, that is how they currently exist in the archive, most of which is cataloged according to Hall's original files. Seldom are exact dates given, but a rough chronology emerges when images are attached to specific projects or trips overseas. Hall also used his Minox less in the late 1960s than at the beginning of the decade. The majority of the images here were taken by Hall, but even those he may not have taken are unattributed (one exception being Marshall Williams's images in Chicago ca. 1965). This is to acknowledge that there is a double decontextualization in effect here: there is Hall's own desire to aggregate the visual material into patterned groups (thus detaching them from specific dates and names) and my own selections of images based on evident genres—lines of people, crowds, intimate conversations, interiors—and certain other alluring details.

In addition to being partial, I have selected images that resonate with the argument advanced in the introductory essay. This argument involves the notion of environmental conditioning broadly speaking; accordingly, images that feature buildings and other environmental hardware are presented here, as are images that illustrate the visual and material aspects of Hall's practices: equipment, graph sheets, and perforated note cards. First pages of notational reports are shown on their own, as are note cards with little corresponding information and unlabeled drawings and graphics. But while these images might support an argument in an allusive and oblique way, they are offered here more as provocation than confirmation. They cannot provide proof, as their proper content is always metonymically deferred—constantly shifting from one medium to the next, from notation to photo to illustration to text. In other words, we should not expect to see what Hall saw in these photos, diagrams, charts, and columns full of numerical abstractions. The images here represent a sampling of attempts to capture the flickering emergence of the human at the intersections of subjectivity and environmentality.

In addition to supporting an argument, I hope that my curatorial presence here is assertive enough to defray the monographic emphasis implied by the presentation of a single individual's professional effects. For while Hall's eccentric understanding of interactional space holds this study together, its effectiveness in doing so is premised not upon the singularity of his vision but its multiplicity. The primary interest of Hall's vast collection of correspondence and images—and what drew me to it beginning around 2015—is not the archive's exclusivity of authorship but the comingling there of many disciplinary strands, from the ethological to the architectural. In this sense, Hall is less a privileged authorial presence than a kind of cipher around which gather heterogenous intellectual, aesthetic, and material patterns. In other words, those who come here seeking the figure of Hall himself might be disappointed to find only his backgrounds.

Series 1
Images of Edward T. Hall and Mildred Reed Hall,
along with ephemera relating to their publications
and consulting business.

Edward T. Hall and Mildred Reed Hall, around 1978.

Like many spouses during this period, Mildred Reed Hall, who had a degree in sociology from Barnard College, was often acknowledged as a kind of secretary/editor for her husband. We can speculate, however, that her role in the development of proxemics was more active than this label implied. While her contributions are difficult to track precisely, it is clear that she facilitated the work of the Edward T. Hall Associates consultancy. Additionally, she would be credited as coauthor of *The Fourth Dimension in Architecture* (1975) and many of their firm's later publications on conducting business overseas.

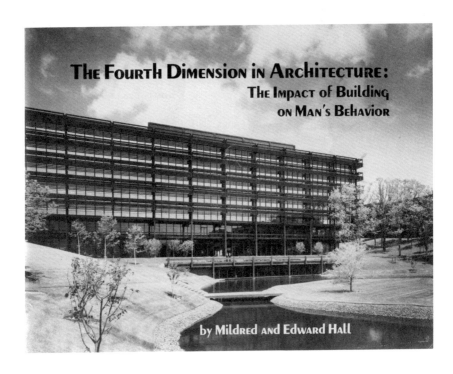

The Fourth Dimension in Architecture:
The Impact of Building on Man's Behavior

by Mildred and Edward Hall

THE SILENT LANGUAGE

EDWARD T. HALL

An anthropologist reveals how we communicate by our manners and behavior

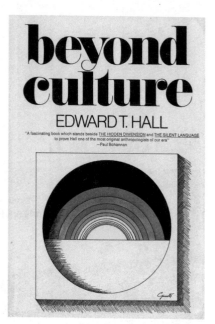

beyond culture

EDWARD T. HALL

"A fascinating book which stands beside THE HIDDEN DIMENSION and THE SILENT LANGUAGE to prove Hall one of the most original anthropologists of our era"
—Paul Bohannan

The Hidden Dimension

Edward T. Hall
Author of THE SILENT LANGUAGE

An anthropologist examines man's use of space in public and in private

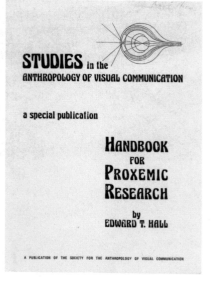

STUDIES in the ANTHROPOLOGY OF VISUAL COMMUNICATION

a special publication

HANDBOOK FOR PROXEMIC RESEARCH

by
EDWARD T. HALL

A PUBLICATION OF THE SOCIETY FOR THE ANTHROPOLOGY OF VISUAL COMMUNICATION

EDWARD T. HALL ASSOCIATES
P.O. BOX 5278
SANTA FE. NEW MEXICO 87501

CLIENT LIST - BUILDING & DESIGN PROJECTS

Bay Area Rapid Transit, San Francisco, California

Boston Floating Hospital

Building Program Associates, San Francisco

Chestnut Lodge, Rockville, Maryland

Chloethiel Woodard Smith & Associates, Washington, D. C.

Educational Facilities Laboratories, Inc., New York

Harvard Business School

International Business Machines, New York

Nixon, Brown, Brokaw, Bowen, Boulder, Colorado

Perkins & Will, Chicago

Philadelphia Geriatrics Center

School Environments Research Project, University of Michigan

Skidmore, Owings and Merrill, Chicago

United States Bureau of Standards

University of Utah, Department of Architecture

Vincent Kling Associates, Philadelphia

Each country has its own chemistry of relationships and its own way of conducting business with special rules for handling time and meeting deadlines, for setting boundaries and arranging spaces. It has rules for bargaining and conducting negotiations just as it has rules for advertising and image building. Each country also has its own rules for organizational behavior; for status and how it is perceived and acknowledged, for handling subordinates and for relating to colleagues and superiors.

WHO WE ARE

Edward T. Hall pioneered the field of intercultural communications with his best sellers, *The Silent Language, The Hidden Dimension,* and *Beyond Culture.* His books are widely read and have been translated into a dozen foreign languages. For more than twenty years Edward T. Hall Associates has worked with clients to improve their performance overseas. Our goal is to maximize productivity, using wherever possible the client's own resources and experience.

Today many countries have large subgroups of different national and ethnic backgrounds, "guest workers" and immigrants. Many multinational corporations employ personnel of diverse nationality and backgrounds. We offer consultation to organizations serving different ethnic groups or employing personnel of different backgrounds.

OUR CLIENTS

Ansul Company, Marinette, Wisconsin
Bay Area Rapid Transit, San Francisco, California
Business Council for International Understanding
Federal Bureau of Investigation
Foreign Service Institute,
    U.S. Department of State
General Electric
Girl Scouts of America
IBM
INSTEP
Louis Harris Associates
McKinsey Foundation
Mobil
Parker Pen
Playback Associates

This is a representative sample over the past twenty years, not a complete list.

The Halls produced these brochures around 1974 for individuals conducting business overseas and designers, two of the firm's primary client groups. Hall was clearly unafraid to exploit the same tropes of cultural difference that his work attempted to demystify.

REPRESENTATIVE CLIENT LIST*

The Ansul Company
Marinette, Wisconsin

Bay Area Rapid Transit
San Francisco, California

Bertrand Goldberg Associates
Chicago, Illinois

Boston Floating Hospital

Building Program Associates
San Francisco, California

Chestnut Lodge
Rockville, Maryland

Cloethiel Woodard Smith & Associates
Washington, D.C.

Educational Facilities Laboratories, Inc.
New York, New York

Harvard Business School

IBM, New York World's Fair Exhibit

Lawrence Halprin Associates
New York, New York

Mobile Oil Company
New York, New York

Nixon, Brown, Brokaw, Bowen
Boulder, Colorado

Perkins & Will
Chicago, Illinois

Skidmore, Owings and Merrill
Chicago, Illinois

United States Bureau of Standards

University of Michigan
School Environments Research Project

University of Utah
Department of Architecture

Vincent Kling Associates
Philadelphia, Pennsylvania

*This is a representative sample of clients over the
past twenty years and is not a complete list.

E. T. Hall Associates
642 Camino Lejo
Santa Fe, New Mexico 87501
505/982-3203

EDWARD T. HALL
ASSOCIATES

CONSULTANTS TO
Architects
Designers
Engineers
Planners

642 Camino Lejo
Santa Fe, N. M. 87501

DESCRIPTION OF SERVICES

Architects, builders, designers and planners all influence people in deep and subtle ways. The success of their designs for housing, office buildings and entire communities depends on people's reactions.

How can you know how people will react? How can you know what people will do in the spaces you create?

The complexity of designing buildings to meet people's needs requires expert advice. Edward T. Hall pioneered the field of proxemics, man's use of space, with the publication of his bestseller, **The Hidden Dimension.** For more than two decades, Edward T. Hall Associates has helped clients determine how occupants will live or work in buildings or communities. There is a way to determine how people will use or react to your built environment at both the unconscious and conscious level. Working with designers during the programmatic phase, data is presented on the needs of occupants based on social, economic, organizational, and cultural factors. This human needs approach helps create environments that enhance people's performance and their sense of well-being.

Clients are assisted in developing procedures to assure maximum use of their personnel and financial resources. This collaboration is based on the client's design expertise and the consultant's knowledge of the needs of the people and organizations who will occupy the buildings. Previous clients have included engineers and architects throughout the United States with projects in mass transit, education, housing (both public and private), medical facilities and offices for business and city government. It is often possible to provide the architect-designer with human factors data to justify desirable solutions which might be rejected if cost alone were the deciding factor.

THREE TYPICAL PROJECTS

Bay Area Rapid Transit, San Francisco.

Consultants to Wurster, Bernardi, and Emmons, Public Structures, Inc., San Francisco. Preparation of report on human needs in design of mass transit systems focusing on: traffic flow in stations and platforms; lighting and signing; noise and visual pollution; seating arrangements; boarding and exiting behavior; analysis of factors in other transit systems leading to stress.

Public Housing Project, St. Louis.

Consultants to Skidmore, Owings, and Merrill, Chicago, taskforce to revitalize a large scale housing project. Prepared report on relationship between design and tenants in existing housing which had been largely abandoned due to tenant dissatisfaction. Analysis of factors included: design criteria; tenant mix; transportation system, and education and community recreational facilities. Throughout period of review, worked with local community and tenants, as well as with outside experts in economics and planning, and with four architectural firms in St. Louis.

Deere and Company, Moline, Illinois.

Five year study of Saarinen's Administrative Center for Deere. The results of this study were published as a monograph: "The Fourth Dimension in Architecture: The Impact of Building on Man's Behavior". This study traced the influence of the building on Deere employees over a five year period and also dealt with the setting as a determinant of behavior and the impact of the building on the industry and on the company's public image.

Series 2
Undated images from an
envelope labeled "Smoking
Gestures." Judging by the
subjects' clothing and Hall's
itinerary, these may have
been taken at Bennington
College in the late 1940s.
These images show Hall paying
attention to interactions
that would later inform his
theories of proxemics.

Hall's photographs taken primarily with his Minox camera in the United States and abroad starting in the late 1950s. Some were organized in boxes with locations labeled, others stored loose. Duplicate prints sometimes appear in more than one location in the files.

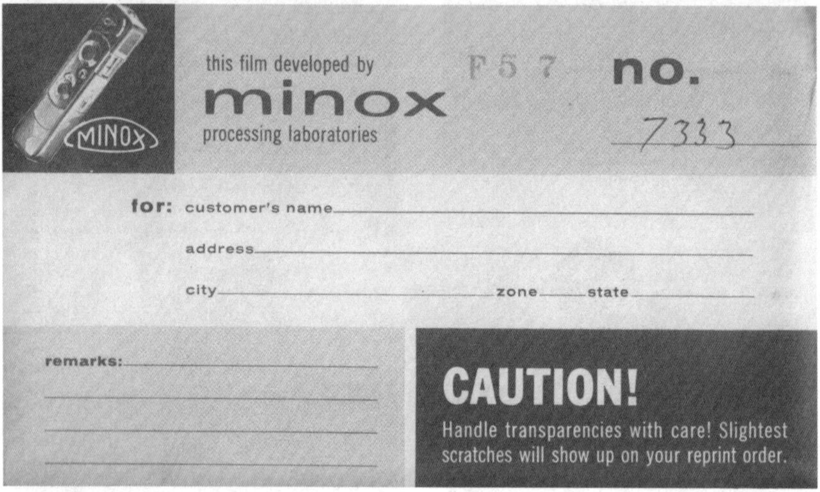

this film developed by **F 5 7** **no.**

minox
processing laboratories

7333

for: customer's name

address

city   zone   state

remarks:

CAUTION!
Handle transparencies with care! Slightest scratches will show up on your reprint order.

Minox was the proprietary service that processed the tiny negatives exposed in the camera, each of which measured 8 × 11 mm. The company returned photographs to Hall in envelopes like these.

Hall saw proxemic bubbles imposing not only in person-to-person interactions but also through the use of "extensions" such as the automobile.

In some images, background environmental features relate to, or even determine, subject behavior. Here, window mullions echo and structure the spacing of individuals.

OC 180

This sequence of color slides was taken on one of Mildred and Edward Hall's trips to Greece for Constantinos Doxiadis's Delos cruises, most likely in 1964. In them, Hall subjects the proxemic attitudes of fellow attendees to the same analysis he applied to the locals in Athens.

Series 4

Ordered groupings of images from the early to mid-1960s that Hall curated for the 1978 exhibition *Architecture as Media*. The image labels convey his thinking about personal and national variation in distancing and about the use of extensions.

#1   INTIMATE DISTANCE indicating close
      relationship in different settings.

      3 photographs

#2 CLOSE PERSONAL DISTANCE almost intimate
in U.S.. Read as close relationship or
confidential or involving subject matter.

5 photographs

#3.   PERSONAL DISTANCE in a business or
professional setting or witn a professional
stance.
5 photographs

#4   PERSONAL DISTANCES

Where the subject matter or the
emotions are not read as
involving.

\-\-

Many of the photo groupings in this series correspond to Hall's categorization of personal space
into four types: intimate, personal, social, and public. In this set, subjects maintain personal
distance without the affective charge of intimate distance.

--

#5 SOCIAL CONSULTATION with the props.

(Note bridging in two instances)

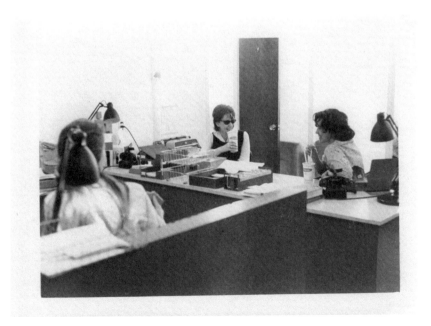

#19 CAN YOU IDENTIFY THE TWO CULTURES?

Nos. 1-4 Greek
Nos. 5-7 English

#14 PEOPLE AND TOWNS clustered similarly

2 photographs

#17   CUEING IS CULTURE SPECIFIC: The examples
      recorded in London, Paris and Washington,
      D.C. contain a wealth of information.

      5 photographs

#18 CUEING BEHAVIOR IN WASHINGTON, D.C.

In general people do not violate the
personal distances to strangers. Study
these photos and pick out those who are
acquainted from those who are not.
No. 1: when sidewalks are wide, people
will space. Note woman who saw the
photographer. Nos. 2-4: taken way beyond
the "Minox involvement distance" and still
contains a wealth of information. Nos. 5-7:
are excellent examples of the intrusion zone
as a function of context. In 5 and 6 it is
roughly 5 1/2' or the height of the body.
Much closer than this when only two or three
people are present it threatening in the
U.S.

#20   THERE"S MORE VARIETY IN A VIRUS

1 photograph

Series 5

Graphic visualizations of proxemic principles, including naturalistic illustrations, media images, altered photos, and schematic diagrams. The diagrams were prepared for Hall's 1966 book *The Hidden Dimension*, though not all appeared in the published version.

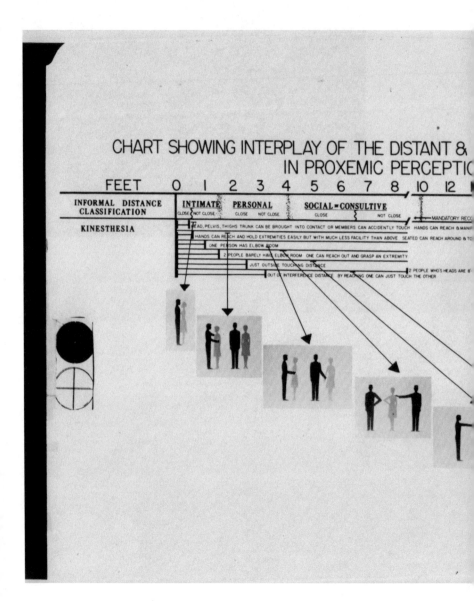

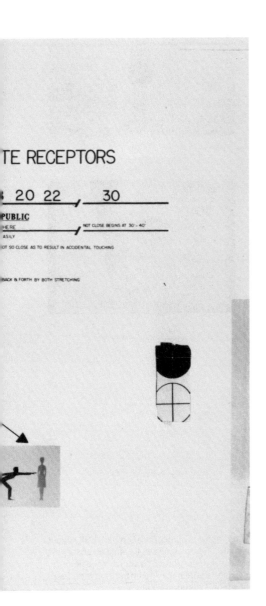

TE RECEPTORS

20 22 / 30

PUBLIC
HERE / NOT CLOSE BEGINS AT 30' - 40'
ASILY

OT SO CLOSE AS TO RESULT IN ACCIDENTAL TOUCHING

BACK & FORTH BY BOTH STRETCHING

In this sequence of illustrations (of which only photographic reproductions remain), Hall sought to capture the visual component of proximity. The distant figure stands well within an observer's foveal field while the observer's peripheral vision creates distortion at the edges of the field. The result is akin to a bubble of vision that the advancing figure begins to fill until his face warps to fit its form. Hall likely produced this set of images for his corporate clients.

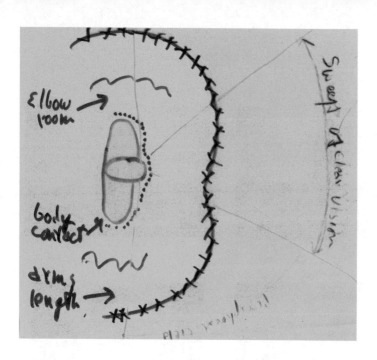

Elbow room →

Body contact →

arms length →

Sweep of clear vision

peripheral field

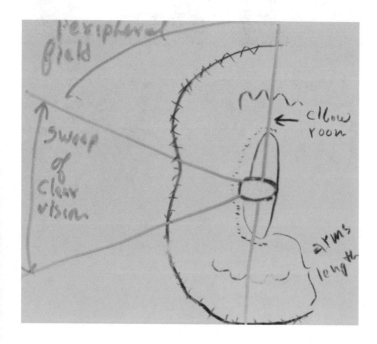

peripheral field

sweep of clear vision

← Elbow room

arms length

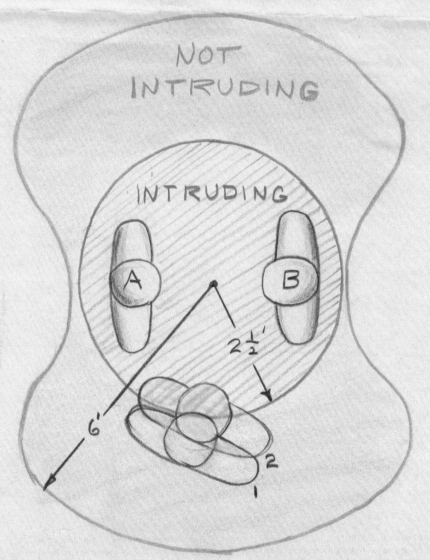

In several illustrations, Hall attempted to portray the proxemic sphere comprising perceptual phenomena—vision, touch, and so on. This image—clearly sketched by a more skilled hand than Hall's—suggests that Black people are more willing than white people to enter into a companion's intimate olfactory bubble. What Hall might have intended as a demonstration of cultural relativism actually ossifies and reinforces stereotypes, illustrating the ironic racial dynamics of proxemics.

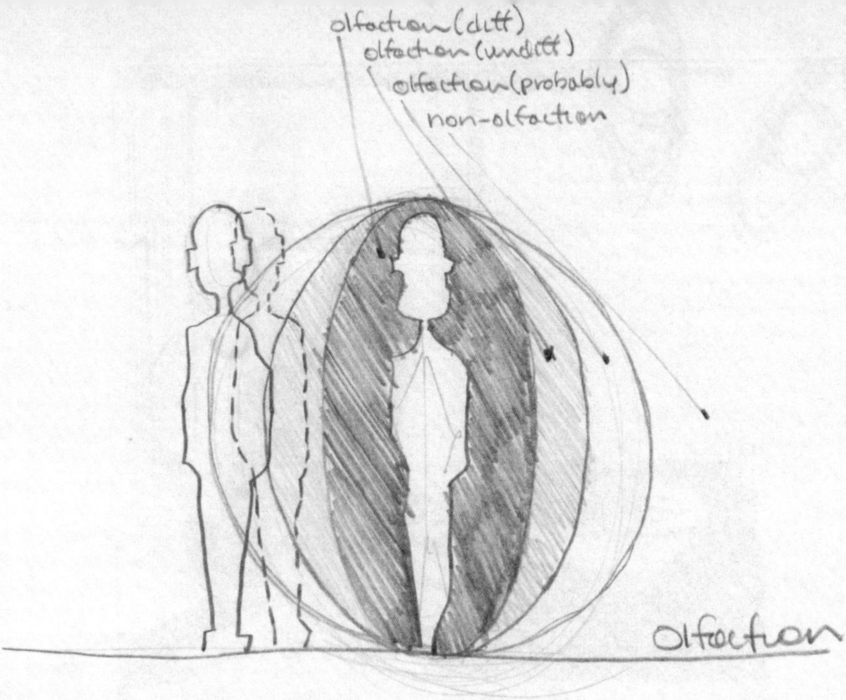

olfaction (diff)
olfaction (undiff)
olfaction (probably)
non-olfaction

olfaction

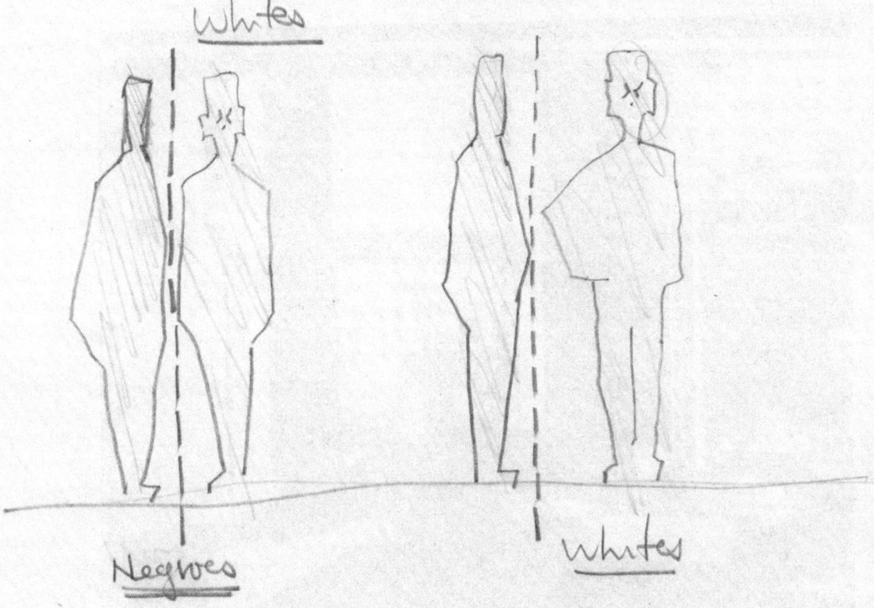

Whites

Negroes

Whites

Kinesthetic

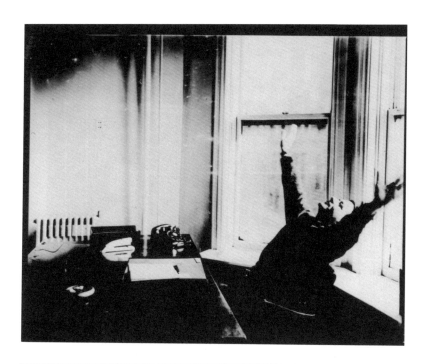

With this series of manipulated photographs Hall seemed to be trying to capture the ergonomics of a work space. The reversals of figure and ground indicate there was no negative space in this environment. Hall implied that extensions and the proxemic bubble of the subject were filling the apparently empty space with very real—if unseen—forces.

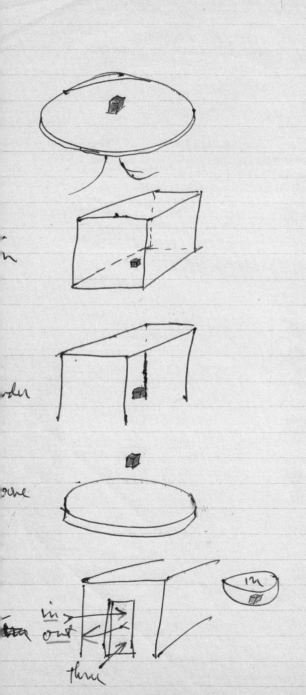

mal

in

oder

ove

in

in
out

thru

"activity built up"---

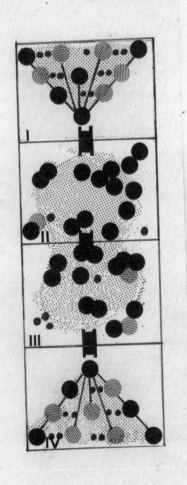

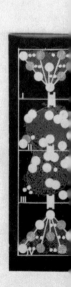

EDWARD I.

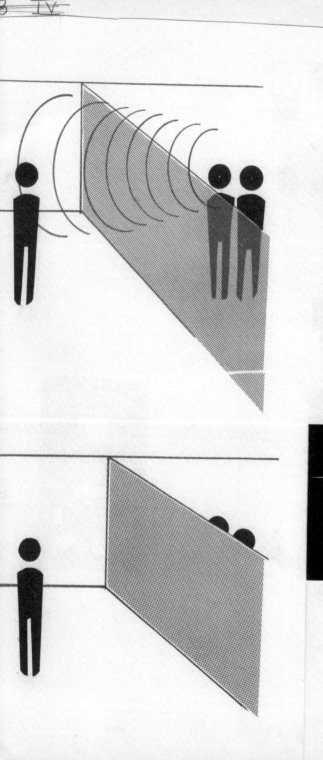

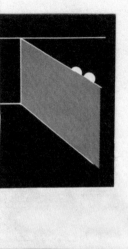

marginal
photo

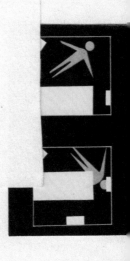

photo

(20)

From *The Hidden Dimension*: "When Westerners think and talk about space, they mean the distance between objects. In the West, we are taught to perceive and to react to the arrangements of objects and to think of space as 'empty.' The meaning of this becomes clear only when it is contrasted with the Japanese, who are trained to give *meaning* to spaces—to perceive the shape and arrangements of spaces; for this they have a word, *ma*." See Hall, *The Hidden Dimension*, 142–143.

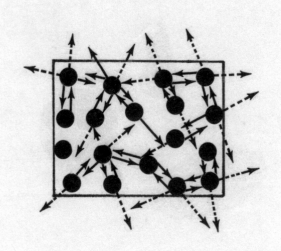

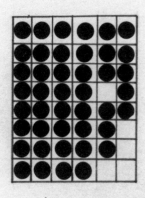

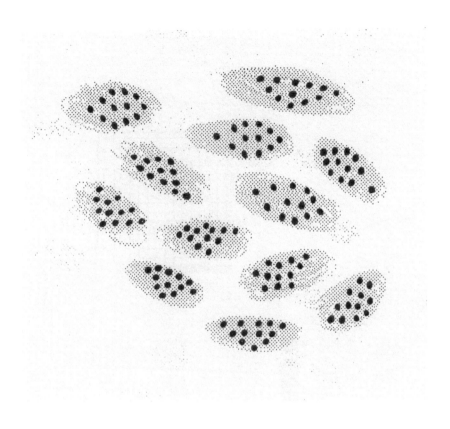

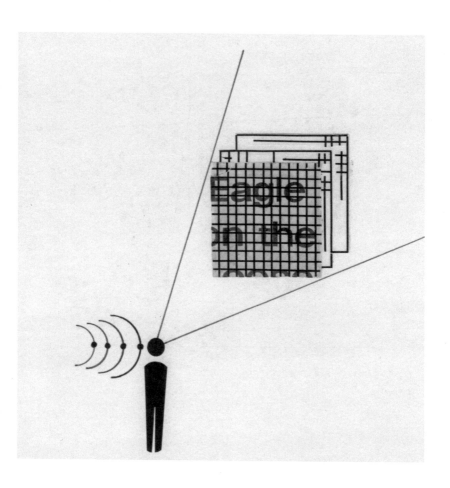

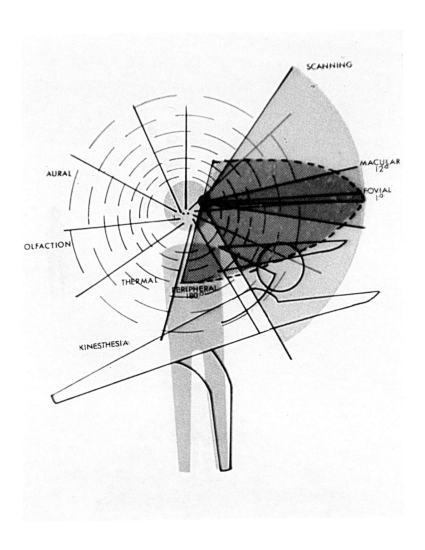

SCANNING

MACULAR
12°

FOVIAL
1.0°

AURAL

PERIPHERAL
180.0°

OLFACTION

THERMAL

KINESTHESIA

155

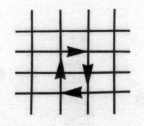

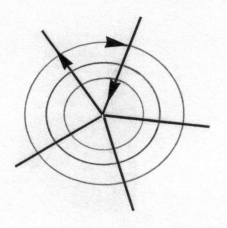

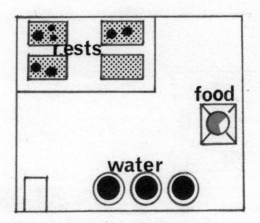

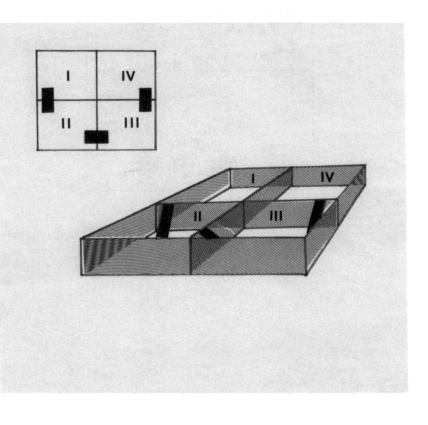

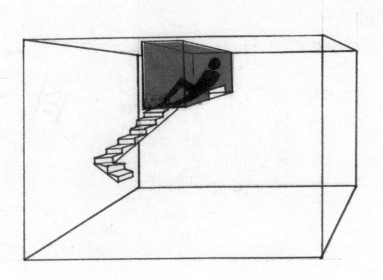

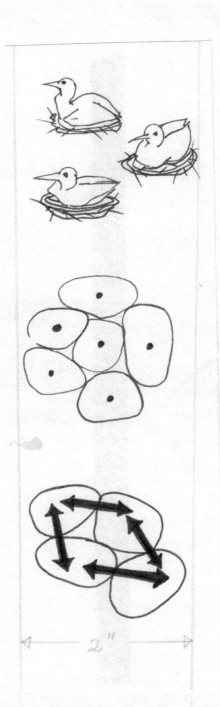

2"

Series 6
An eclectic selection of visual materials, from photos of
animals to media images both manipulated and unaltered. These
were generated contemporaneously in the early to mid-1960s.

Serge Boutourline Jr. hangs pictures on a large board covered with media clippings.
The photo appears to be from the mid-1960s, a time Hall was collecting much of the press
clippings and advertising material preserved in the archive.

Secretary of State Dulles with President Eisenhower, 1955.

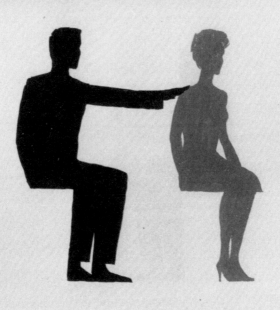

TWO OUTLOOKS—Budget Director Kermit Gordon, left, vis-à-vis Chairman Wilbur D. Mills of the House Ways and Means Committee

...MAIS PAS
TOUT A FAIT DE
LA MÊME
MANIÈRE :
ARTHUR AU
COIN DU FEU,
MARILYN

Elle avait
rencontré José
à Mexico où elle achetait
des meubles. Ce fut
le coup de foudre. Il est
venu pour elle
48 heures
à Hollywood.

ILO panorama

Published by the International Labor Office, Geneva
Number 23   March-April 1967

International Institute for Labor Studies

By Harry Naltchayan, Staff Photographer

SHARING SMILES: The ladies cornered some of the greetings at the Jordan dinner yesterday. Mrs. Yusuf Haikal (far left) welcomes Mrs. Majid Khadduri. In the background (left to right) are U. S. Envoy William Macomber, Jordan's Ambassador Yusuf Haikal and Prof. Khadduri.

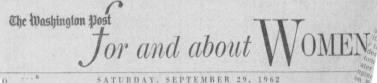

The Washington Post

for and about WOMEN

0 ...R SATURDAY, SEPTEMBER 29, 1962

173

TREASURY—Douglas Dillon has been kept busy with the problems of budget balancing. Here he chats with Walter W. Heller, left, head of the Council of Economic Advisers.

22

N Y times mg 11/5/61
1 col 12"

Personal   (not Close)

(note Dillon's hand inside contact zone)

JSTICE—Robert F. Kennedy, here conferring in his shirt sleeves with Deputy Attorney ...neral Byron R. White, recently completed a Midwestern tour studying organized crime.

ALL THE GABORS

It's reunion time again for the Gabors in their native Vienna. The sisters, Eva, Magda and Zsa Zsa (left), chat in a tiny group as Mama Jolie (right) talks with their father, Vilmos Gabor, at the annual family get-together. Mr. Gabor, 80, makes his home in Budapest and was permitted by Hungarian Communist police to travel to Austria for the occasion.—AP Wirephoto.

Media images appear to have been photographed and cut out so that the distances between figures could be manipulated to change the meaning of their interactions. What might appear as a business transaction within the social register of proximity would appear completely otherwise if the figures were pushed together into the intimate bubble. (This rather strange material is undated, and Hall never mentions it in his notes or correspondence.)

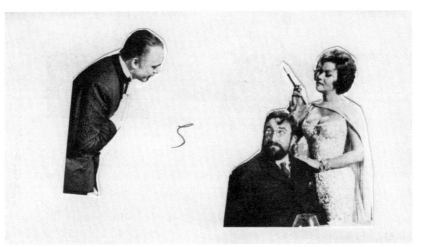

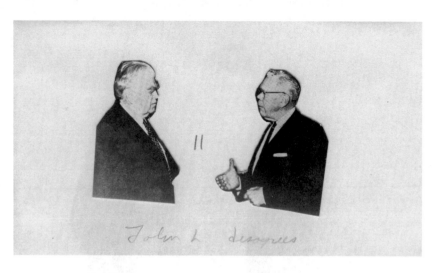

BREHON McFARLAND CONGRATULATES HIS GIRL

FOVIAL VISION

These juxtapositions of animal and human behavior reveal sociobiological assumptions that Hall was never able to break free from completely.

Series 7

Documents related to Hall's experiments at the Illinois
Institute of Technology (IIT), which constitute his only
attempt to formalize and verify the proxemic notation
system. While initially limited to the analysis of the job
interview skills of a group described by Hall as "working
class blacks" (WCB) in a mock office space/observation
room, the study soon expanded to include the analysis
of researchers themselves, photographs taken in the field,
and design of complex apparatuses for the viewing and
interpretation of documentary evidence.

At the heart of these conflicting and ambiguous documents
rests the category of race. At the philosophical level,
proxemics was meant to demonstrate the artificiality of the
category; that external cultural structures, not genetic or
biological attributes, determined behaviors and perceptions.
But the logic of racial difference—specifically Black/white
difference—nonetheless structured the study at the deepest
levels. Though he failed to acknowledge it explicitly,
it becomes clear in reading Hall's own account that what
he described as "standard average European-American" (SAE)
culture was the scale against which other groups' use of
micro-space was being compared (and in which the "WCB"
under observation were implicitly not included). In such
a perspective, the paradoxical project of proxemics comes
into focus: to locate a mythic human universality via the
obsessive analysis of difference.

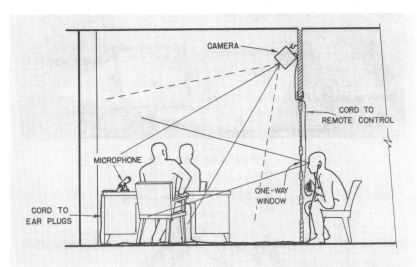

Figure 3. Interview office showing placement of camera and observer.

One of the research subjects has taken on the role of research observer, sitting outside the model office holding the camera shutter release. Hall felt that *when* observers chose to snap a meaningful event said a great deal about their proxemic frames.

Figure 6. Camera-equipped panel t

200

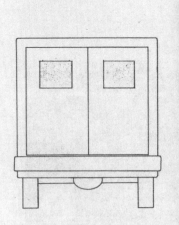

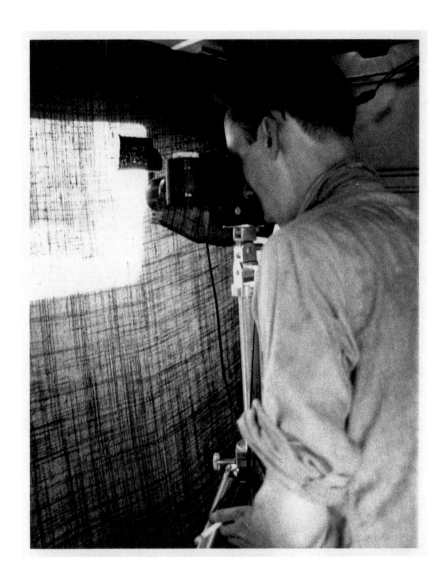

The "mobile blind" allowed Hall to transfer the observational dynamics of his model office to the street. He did not account, however, for the ways in which this change of context would impact the variables of the experiment. For instance, the interactional situations observed would not be predefined, and, most significantly, subjects would not be aware they were being observed.

In this sequence the street corner and traffic signal post seem to provide a stage and frame for various configurations of groups and individuals. These determinative elements seem to accompany otherwise solitary figures.

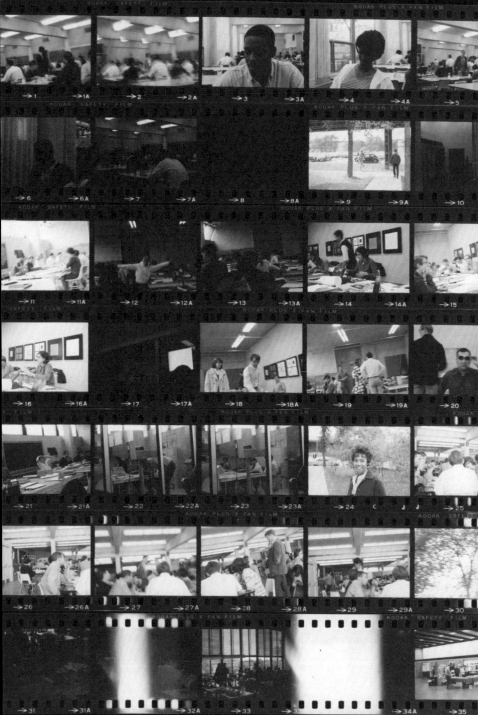

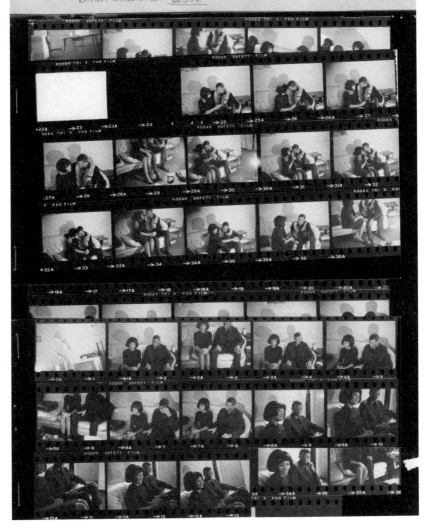

These contact sheets collect images taken by Marshall Williams, one of Hall's research assistants and a design student at IIT. As an African American, Williams was able to enter and study the more intimate spaces of domestic interaction between Black subjects.

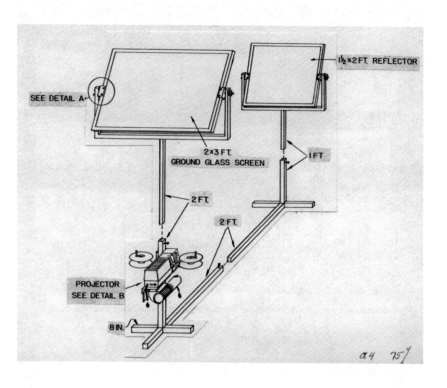

SEE DETAIL A

1½×2 FT. REFLECTOR

2×3 FT.
GROUND GLASS SCREEN

1 FT.

2 FT.

2 FT.

PROJECTOR
SEE DETAIL B

8 IN.

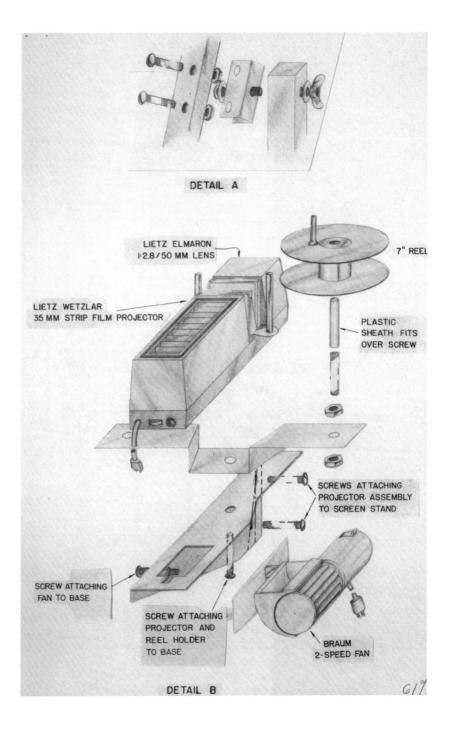

DETAIL A

LIETZ ELMARON
1·2,8 / 50 MM LENS

LIETZ WETZLAR
35 MM STRIP FILM PROJECTOR

7" REEL

PLASTIC
SHEATH FITS
OVER SCREW

SCREWS ATTACHING
PROJECTOR ASSEMBLY
TO SCREEN STAND

SCREW ATTACHING
FAN TO BASE

SCREW ATTACHING
PROJECTOR AND
REEL HOLDER
TO BASE

BRAUM
2-SPEED FAN

DETAIL B

617

217

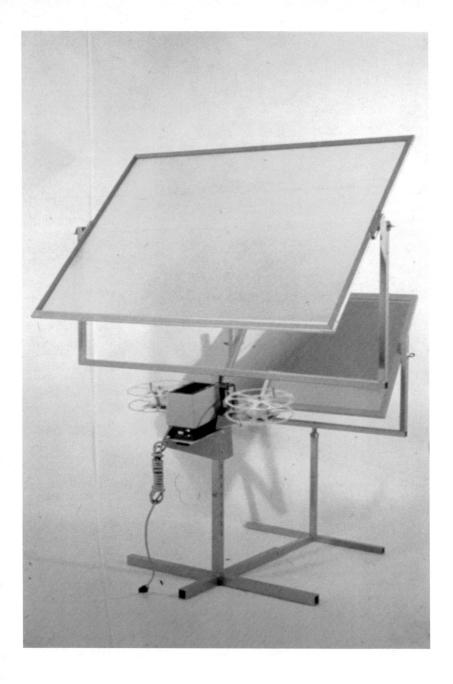

Hall constructed a special device to immerse the proxemicist in the photograph. Still photographs developed on film strips could be viewed while the surrounding circumstances were occluded. Hall believed this arrangement could eliminate not only distractions but other types of bias as well.

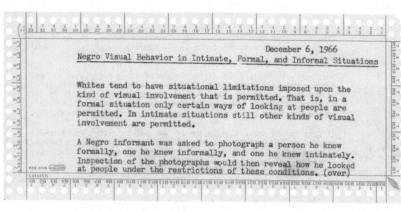

December 6, 1966

Negro Visual Behavior in Intimate, Formal, and Informal Situatioms

Whites tend to have situational limitations imposed upon the
kind of visual involvement that is permitted. That is, in a
formal situation only certain ways of looking at people are
permitted. In intimate situations still other kinds of visual
involvement are permitted.

A Negro informant was asked to photograph a person he knew
formally, one he knew informally, and one he knew intimately.
Inspection of the photographs would then reveal how he looked
at people under the restrictions of these conditions. (over)

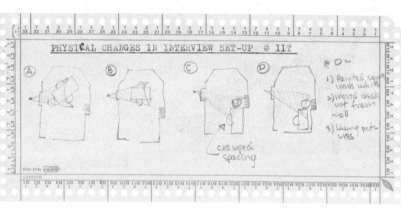

PHYSICAL CHANGES IN INTERVIEW SET-UP @ IIT

Dr. Hall recommended the following aspects to be considered for an interview situation (job interview):

1. How long is a Negro expected to be interviewed for a semi-skilled job?
2. What is the significance of the waiting period ?
3. What kind of fundamental discrepencies are there between Negroes and Whites?
4. Are pauses very important?
5. How long are they?
6. What significance has a desk? Where to put the chairs?
7. What kind of a set-up would be ideal for an interview observer?

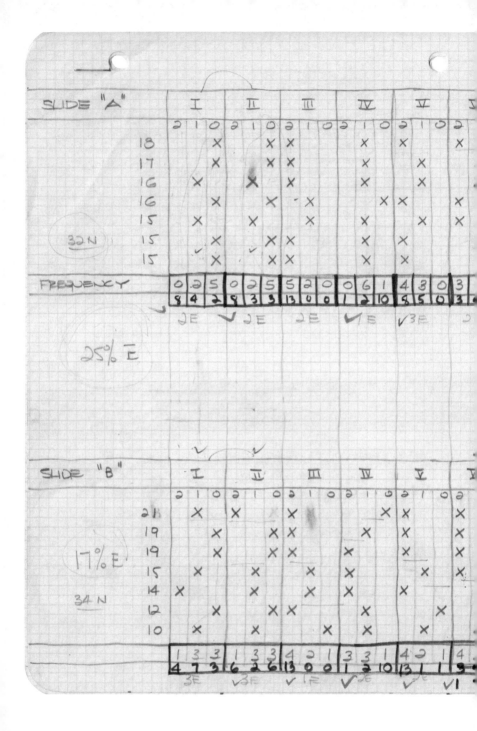

Negro Subjects—

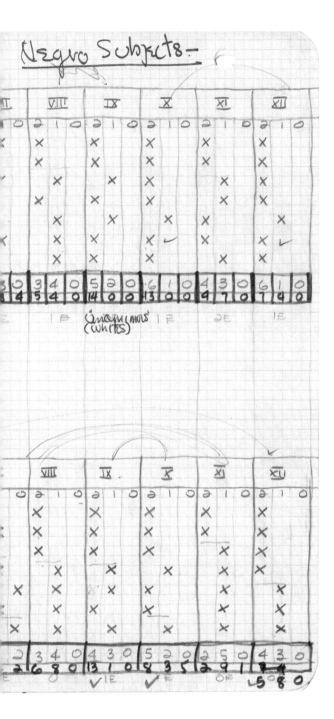

II			VII			IX			X			XI			XII		
0	2	1	0	2	1	0	2	1	0	2	1	0	2	1	0	2	1	0
	×			×			×			×			×	
	×			×			×			×			×	
		×			×		×				×		×
	×			×			×				×		×
		×			×			×		×	×				×
×			×			×	✓		×				×	✓
	×			×			×				×	

| 3 | 4 | 0 | 5 | 2 | 0 | 6 | 1 | 0 | 4 | 3 | 0 | 6 | 1 | 0 |
| 4 | 5 | 4 | 0 | 14 | 0 | 0 | 13 | 0 | 0 | 9 | 7 | 0 | 7 | 4 | 0 |

1 E unanimous (whites) 1 E 2 E 1 E

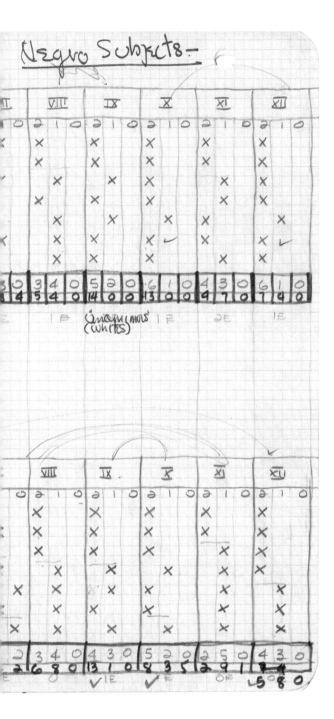

VIII			IX			X			XI			XII		
0	2	1	0	2	1	0	2	1	0	2	1	0	2	1	0
×			×			×			×			×	
×			×			×			×			×	
×			×			×				×		×
	×		×			×				×		×
×		×		×			×				×	
×		×		×			×			×	
×		×		×			×			×	

3	4	0	4	3	0	5	2	0	2	5	0	4	3	0
2	6	8	0	13	1	0	8	3	5	2	9	1	7	4
E		✓ 1 E		✓ E		0 E		5	8	0

223

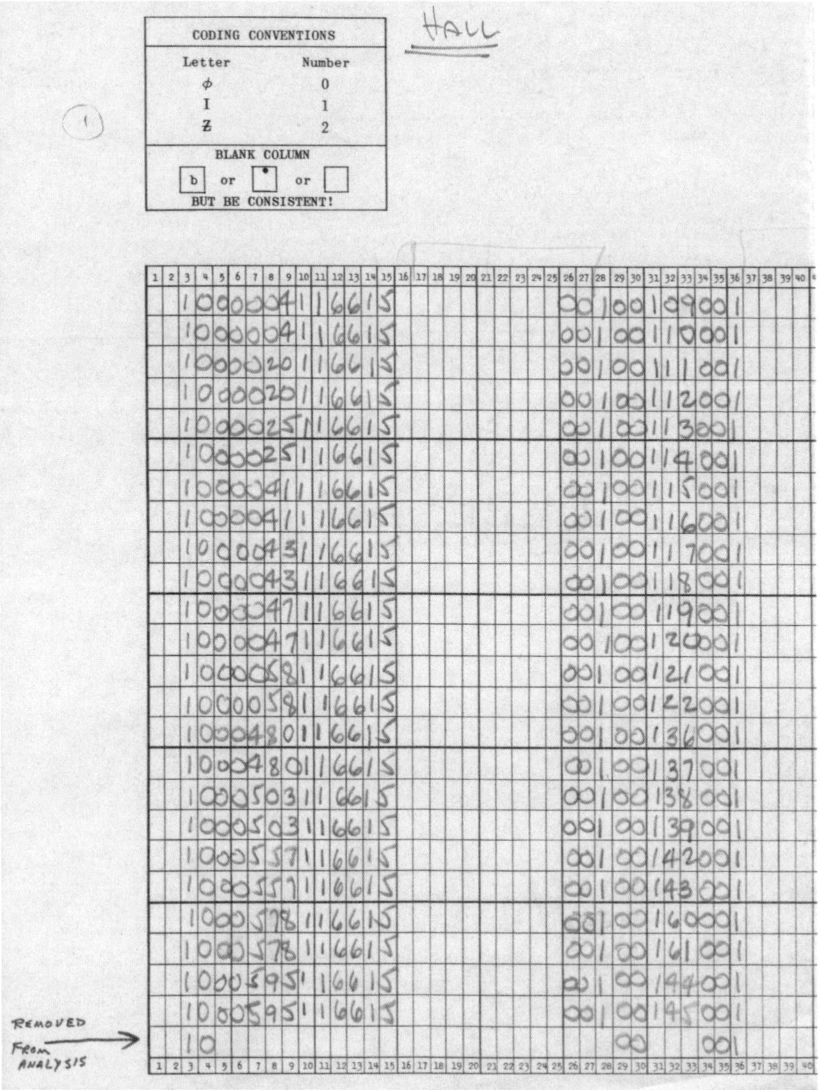

CODING CONVENTIONS	
Letter	Number
ϕ	0
I	1
Z	2
BLANK COLUMN	
b or · or ☐	
BUT BE CONSISTENT!	

(1)

1 2 3 4 5 6 7 8 9 10 11 12 13 14 15	16 17 18 19 20 21 22 23 24 25	26 27 28 29 30 31 32 33 34 35 36 37 38 39 40
1 000041 1 6615		00 100 109 00 1
1 000041 1 6615		001 00 110 00 1
1 000020 1 6615		00 100 111 00 1
1 000020 1 6615		00 100 112 00 1
1 000025 1 6615		00 100 113 00 1
1 000025 1 6615		00 100 114 00 1
1 000041 1 6615		00 100 115 00 1
1 000041 1 6615		00 100 116 00 1
1 000043 1 6615		00 100 117 00 1
1 000043 1 6615		00 100 118 00 1
1 000047 1 6615		00 100 119 00 1
1 000047 1 6615		00 100 120 00 1
1 000058 1 6615		001 00 121 00 1
1 000058 1 6615		001 00 122 00 1
1 000480 1 6615		001 00 136 00 1
1 000480 1 6615		00 100 137 00 1
1 000503 1 6615		00 100 138 00 1
1 000503 1 6615		001 00 139 00 1
1 000557 1 6615		00 100 142 00 1
1 000557 1 6615		00 100 143 00 1
1 000578 1 6615		00 100 160 00 1
1 000578 1 6615		00 100 161 00 1
1 000595 1 6615		00 100 144 00 1
1 000595 1 6615		00 100 145 00 1
1 0		00 001

REMOVED FROM ANALYSIS →

224

HEAD	SLOPE	1	The person has his head sloped backward.
		2	The person has his head sloped forward.
		3	The person has his head sloped sideways.
	EYES	4	The person is looking in Zone 1.
		5	The person is looking in Zone 2.
		6	The person is looking in Zone 3.
		7	The person is looking in Zone 4.
		8	The person is engaged in eye-to-eye contact.
	FACIAL EXPRESSION	9	You can tell how this person feels from eyebrows.
		10	You can tell how this person feels from forehead.
		11	You can tell how this person feels from eye-lids.
		12	You can tell how this person feels from his mouth.
SHOULDERS	SLOPE	13	This person's shoulders slope to his left.
		14	This person's shoulders slope to his right.
	SQUARED ROUNDED	15	This person's shoulders are squared away.
		16	This person's shoulders are rounded.
ARMS	FOREARM	17	The angle of the person's forearm.
		18	The person has his forearm extended.
		19	The person's forearm is held "in" (or "out").
		20	The person's forearm is "free" (or "resting").
HANDS	PALMS	21	The person's palms are held "in" (or "out").
	FINGERS	22	The person's fingers are extended.
		23	The person's fingers are curled "in."
TRUNK	SLOPE	24	The person's trunk is sloped forward.
		25	The person's trunk is sloped backward.
		26	The person's trunk is sloped sideways.
LEGS	STRAIGHT	27	The person's legs are straight.
		28	The person's legs are straight and crossed.
	EXTENDED	29	The person's legs are extended.
		30	The person's legs are extended and crossed.
	STAND LEG	31	The person is standing on his left leg.
		32	The person is standing on his right leg.
		33	The person is standing on both legs.

The nebulous quality of the work at IIT is not surprising given Hall's ambitious—almost metaphysical—agenda:

The hypothesis of the project—*the use of micro-space in interethnic encounters*—was that the non-verbal cues and distance setting mechanisms of working class blacks (WCB) were different in some respects from those of middle class whites (MCW) in the job interview-gatekeeping situation. However, we did not let the fact that we had a hypothesis to test act as the principal determinant in our research. Our preoccupation was not so much with the proving of a hypothesis as in discovering an authentic situation in which it was possible to observe and record what happened as well as to discover whether two people with different ethnic backgrounds *perceived the same thing or not*.

Despite the abundance of documentation relating to Hall's research in Chicago, the exact mechanics and nature of these experiments remain obscure. Notation charts were made for both white and Black subjects, but white subjects were not officially enlisted as interviewees. (A footnote cryptically informs the reader that "observation of the MCW interview covers the past 30 years....") See Hall, *Handbook for Proxemics Research*, 27, 33.

SLIDE	VERY TENSE	TENSE	NEUTRAL	CALM	VERY CALM
A		卌 IIII	卌 III	II	
B		III	卌 II	III	
C	III	III		II	I
D		卌	卌	III	
E	II	卌	II	II	
F		II	II	卌 I	I
G		卌 II	II	卌 I	
H			III	卌	卌
I	II	卌卌 I		I	
J	卌	II	卌	II	

SLIDE	VERY NERVOUS	NERVOUS	NEUTRAL	RELAXED	VERY RELAXED
A		卌 III	II	III	
B	I	卌	II	卌 I	
C	II	II	II	I	II
D		II	卌 I	卌	
E	I	III		卌	
F		II	III	III	卌 I
G	I	卌 II	III	III	
H			II	卌 III	II
I	II	卌卌 I	II	I	I
J	II	II	卌	II	

SLIDE	VERY LISTENING	LISTENING	NEUTRAL	DAYDREAMING	VERY DAYDREAMING
A	卌 I	卌 III			
B	III	卌	II		
C	III	III	IIII	III	I
D	卌 II	卌 I	I		
E	I	卌 I	卌		
F		II	III	卌 II	I
G		III	III	卌 II	
H		卌 IIII	III		
I	卌 III	卌 I			
J	II	卌 卌	II		

SLIDE	VERY FORMAL	FORMAL	NEUTRAL	INFORMAL	VERY INFORMAL
A		I	II	卌 卌	
B	III	卌 卌			
C	I	I	III	I	卌
D	II	卌 卌	II		
E		I	IIV	卌III	
F			II	I/II	卌 I
G				卌III	卌
H				卌III	卌
I	卌 I	卌 III			
J			卌 I	卌 I	

226

Negro Subjects

7 SAMPLES

I

SLIDE	VERY TENSE	TENSE	NEUTRAL		CALM	VERY CALM	
A			2	2	/|	||	5
B			3	3		//	4
C			2	2	||	||	5
D			4	3		||	4
E			4	3			4
F			5	4			3
G			4	4			3
H			4	4	||		3
I			3	2	||		5
J			3	3			4

II

SLIDE	VERY NERVOUS	NERVOUS	NEUTRAL		RELAXED	VERY RELAXED	
A			2	2	|||	||	4
B			3	3	||		6
C			1	1	||	||	5
D			2	2	|||		5
E			4	2			2
F			5	5			5
G			2	2			1
H			3	3		|||	5
I			3	2			4
J			3	3	||		4

III

SLIDE	VERY LISTENING	LISTENING	NEUTRAL		DAYDREAMING	VERY DAYDREAMING	
A	||	|||	2	2			5
B	||	||	2	2			5
C	|||	|||	0	0			7
D	||		4	3			4
E	||	||||	1	1			6
F			2	1		|||	6
G			2	2			5
H	|||		4	4			3
I	||	||	3	3			4
J		||	4	4			3

IV

SLIDE	VERY FORMAL	FORMAL	NEUTRAL		INFORMAL	VERY INFORMAL	
A			6	4			3
B	|||	||	2	2			5
C			6	3			4
D			4	3			5
E			6	4			4
F			4	3		|||	4
G			4	3			4
H			5	3			4
I	|||		3	3			4
J			7	5			3

Name_____ Age_____ Sex_____ <u>Slide A B C D E</u>
(circle one)

You will be looking at five slides. At first you will see them very quickly, then you will see each slide again. When you see them the second time, answer the following questions. You will not be able to see the slides again. We can't answer any questions.

1. The person I have just seen is:

   a. very nervous_____   c. in-between_____   e. very relaxed_____
   b. rather nervous___   d. rather relaxed___

2. The person I have just seen is:

   a. very confident_____   c. in-between_____   e. very scared_____
   b. rather confident___   d. rather scared___

3. The person I have just seen is:

   a. very friendly_____   c. in-between_____   e. very angry_____
   b. rather friendly___   d. rather angry_____

4. The person I have just seen is:

   a. very interested_____   c. in-between_____   e. very bored_____
   b. rather interested_   d. rather bored___

5. The person I have just seen is:

   a. very serious_____   c. in-between_____   e. very carefree___
   b. rather serious___   d. rather carefree___

6. The person I have just seen is talking to:

   a. a Negro_____   b. a White_____   c. can't tell_____

7. Is there anything important about the person you have just seen that is not listed above? If so explain in your own words below.

PROBLEM: Discovering minimal pairs of kinesic units.

APPROACH: Subjects take photographs of person in interview situation. Photos serve as a reminder system for the subject. Subject then provides the data and the context. Subject should be able to isolate units and define them.

Any other subject, although not familiar with the context, can help isolate minimal units by making distinctions he feels are significant.

DIMENSIONS: Look for minimal pairs in the following areas at the present;

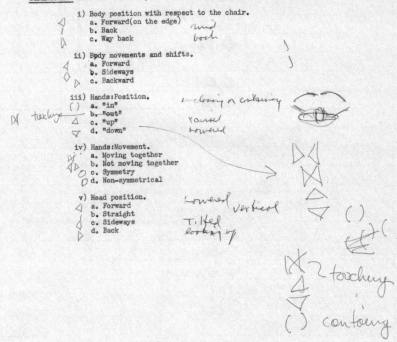

    i) Body position with respect to the chair.
       a. Forward(on the edge)
       b. Back
       c. Way back

    ii) Body movements and shifts.
       a. Forward
       b. Sideways
       c. Backward

    iii) Hands:Position.
       a. "in"
       b. "out"
       c. "up"
       d. "down"

    iv) Hands:Movement.
       a. Moving together
       b. Not moving together
       c. Symmetry
       d. Non-symmetrical

    v) Head position.
       a. Forward
       b. Straight
       c. Sideways
       d. Back

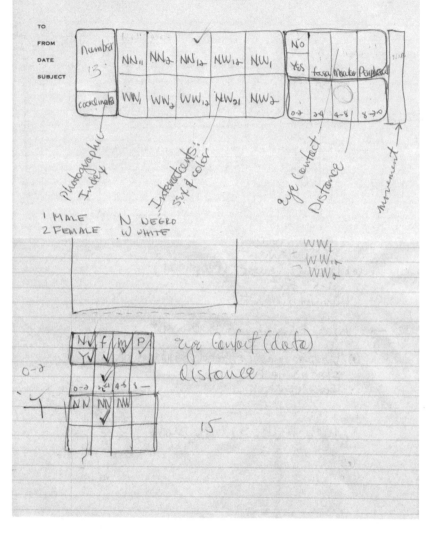

1 MALE   N NEGRO

2 FEMALE   W WHITE

eye Contact (data)

distance

15

① 56 / 1 / 103 / 6 / 11 / 8 / 8 / 4
② 55 / 1 / 22 / 6 / 13 / 8 / 4 / 3
③ 55 / 2 / 11 / 3 / 83 / 1 / 1 / 3 /
④ 55 / 1 / 103 / 6 / 11 / 8 / 8 / 4
⑥ 56 / 4 / 11 / 3 / 33 / 1 / 2 / 3
⑤ 55 / 2 / 202 / 6 / 13 / 8 / 8 / 3
⑦ 56 / 0 / 103 / 6 / 11 / 8 / 3 / 3
⑧ 56 / 0 / 22 / 6 / 11 / 2 / 3 / 3
⑨ ⁰⁾34 / 0 / 303 / 6 / 11 / 8 / 8 / 4
b) 54 / ⁴³ / 101 / 6 / 13 / 2 / 2 / 2³ /
c) 36 / 3 / 303 / 6 / 11 / 8 / 8 / 4

10) 55 / 1 / 103 / 6 / 11 / 8 / 8 / 4 /
11) 55 / 2 / 202 / 6 / 11 / 8 / 8 / 4 /
12) 55 / 1 / 22 / 6 / 11 / 8 / 3 / 3 /
13) 55 / 2 / 22 / 6 / 13 / 8 / 8 / 3
14) 33 / 3 / 103 / 6 / 11 / 8 / 8 / 3

231

FRANK HICKMAN   7-29-64

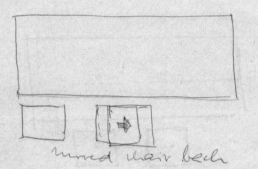

moved chair back

THE SPATIAL RELATIONSHIP

EMPLOYER—NEGRO APPLICANT

DESK—CHAIR

IN AN

INTERVIEW SITUATION

WERE EXAMINED

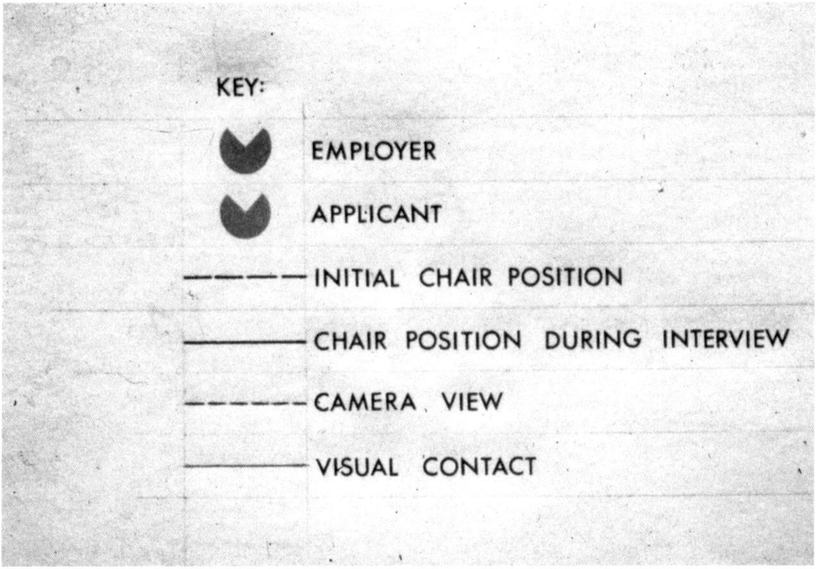

KEY:

⬤ EMPLOYER

⬤ APPLICANT

————— INITIAL CHAIR POSITION

————— CHAIR POSITION DURING INTERVIEW

————— CAMERA VIEW

————— VISUAL CONTACT

```
      PROGRAM DATAGRF(INPUT,OUTPUT)
      INTEGER GRAPH,SYM,VCODE,TFINC,P
      DIMENSION A(300,19),B(300,19),GRAPH(13,100),SYM(4),VCODE(40,19)
      COMMON A,B,IK,M,N,IJ
      DATA (SYM(K),K=1,4)/1H ,1HA,1HB,1HC/
      I=1
      S=1
      READ 8001,TFINC,NPROB
      DO 5000 KPROB=1,NPROB
      READ 8001,KREAD,IK,IJ
      GOTO (9111,9222,9333),KREAD
 9111 CALL READ1
      GOTO 10
 9222 CALL READ2
      GOTO 10
 9333 CALL READ3
   10 CONTINUE
      DO 2000 K=1,10
      DO 2001 L=1,100
      GRAPH(K,L)=SYM(1)
 2001 CONTINUE
 2000 CONTINUE
      DO 3013 J=1,19
      IF (M.EQ.0) GOTO 3013
      NDIF=0
      NHI=0
      PRINT 9000, J
      PRINT 9002
      KV=10
      KF=0
      KT=-99
      KN=N
      IF (KN-100) 3012,3012,3001
 3012 KF=1
      GOTO 3000
 3001 KN=100
 3000 KT=KT+100
      P=0
      DO 3003 I=KT,KN,TFINC
      P=P+1
      IF(M-I) 3004,3005,3005
 3005 L=KV-B(I,J)
      XB=B(I,J)
      XB=SIGN(S,XB)
      IF(XB.NE.-1.0) GRAPH(L,P)=SYM(3)
      K=KV-A(I,J)
      XA=A(I,J)
      XA=SIGN(S,XA)
      IF(XA.EQ.-1.0) GOTO 3003
      IF (K-L) 3014,3007,3006
 3014 NHI=NHI+1
 3006 GRAPH(K,P)=SYM(2)
      NDIF=NDIF+1
      GOTO 3003
 3007 GRAPH(K,P)=SYM(4)
      GOTO 3003
 3004 XA=A(I,J)
```

Hall commissioned a special FORTRAN algorithm to analyze data. In this printout, measurements of "Thermal Code" could be correlated to "Kinesic Isometrism" and so on. Whether digital or analog, however, it becomes apparent that all proxemic schema were incomplete, always in need of qualification. The notations always called for more notations.

E.T. HALL -- PILOT STUDY 1, SPEARMAN R MATRIX -- NEGRO

****

		SYMBOL *** =	0.487 =.01 LEVEL OF SIGNIF
		SYMBOL ** =	0.381 =.05 LEVEL OF SIGNIF
		SYMBOL * =	0.323 =.10 LEVEL OF SIGNIF

		1 KINESI C ISOM ETRISM	2 BODY O RIENTA TION	3 KINESI HETICS CODE	4 RETIN L COM
1	KINESIC ISOMETRISM	1.000	-0.120	0.684 ***	-0.02
2	BODY ORIENTATION	-0.120	1.000	-0.230	0.12
3	KINESTHETICS CODE	0.684 ***	-0.230	1.000	-0.06
4	RETINAL COMB	-0.026	0.121	-0.066	1.00
5	TOUCH CODE	0.451 **	-0.442 **	0.743 ***	-0.04
6	THERMAL CODE	0.389 **	-0.311	0.701 ***	0.07
7	OLFACTION CODE	0.336 *	-0.334 *	0.754 ***	-0.00
8	VOICE LOUD CODE	0.317	0.139	0.305	0.37
9	TOTAL SCORE	0.542 ***	-0.384 **	0.858 ***	-0.05

TWO-TAILED TEST, DF=26
TWO-TAILED TEST, DF=26
TWO-TAILED TEST, DF=26

5 H E	6 THERMA L CODE	7 OLFACT ION CO DE	8 VOICE LOUD C ODE	9 TOTAL SCORE	
51 **	0.389 **	0.336 *	0.317	0.542 ***	Down
42 **	-0.311	-0.334 *	0.139	-0.384 **	Down
43 ***	0.701 ***	0.754 ***	0.305	0.858 ***	UP
49	0.076	-0.002	0.371 *	-0.057	UP
000	0.943 ***	0.758 ***	0.263	0.904 ***	UP
43 ***	1.000	0.729 ***	0.297	0.871 ***	Down
58	0.729 ***	1.000	0.187	0.823 ***	UP
263	0.297	0.187	1.000	0.412 **	UP
004 ***	0.871 ***	0.823 ***	0.412 **	1.000	

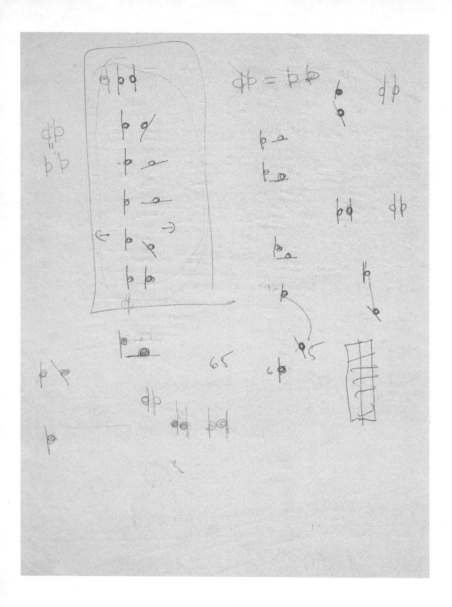

These little pictograms formed an early version of proxemic notation in which the straight line represented the plane formed by a subject's shoulders and the circle represented the head. Quick sketches could capture body posture during a conversation, recording observations such as whether subjects were using angles as a type of defensive distancing.

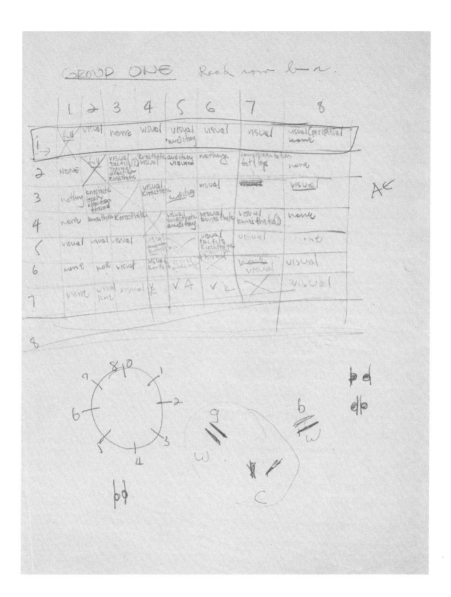

239

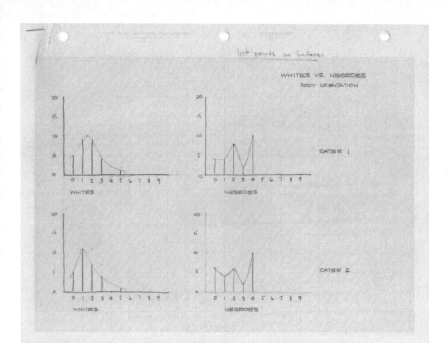

WHITES VS. NEGROES
BODY ORIENTATION

list points as before:

RATER 1

RATER 2

WHITES   NEGROES

14

SUBJECT'S CODE

Column No.	Variable 4 (3)	Description
~~58~~ 64	Lateral displacement (to be used with ~~Col. No. 62~~ ratings 0,4,5, and 9 only in Col. 63)	0-
		1- (overlap of shoulders)
		2- (line up of opposite shoulders)
		3- (one elbow extended)
		4- (one elbow extended - plus)
		5- (two elbows extended)
		6- (one arm extended)
		7- (one arm extended - plus)
		8- (two arms extended)
		9- (two arms extended - plus)

5 (4)

~~60~~ 65	~~Movement: (changing orientation)~~ Change of orientation	0-
		1-
		2-
		3-
		4- closing
		5- no movement
		6- opening
		7-
		8-
		9-

6 (5)

~~61~~ 66	~~Movement: (toward or away from)~~ Change of distance	0-
		1-
		2-
		3-
		4- toward
		5- no movement
		6- away from
		7-
		8-
		9-

Hall documented occasions that saw white and Black people interacting in order to make comparisons. In the chart corresponding to the photographs, Hall isolated and labeled specific groupings and coded their postures. This image also shows Hall experimenting with the tracing technique he was developing.

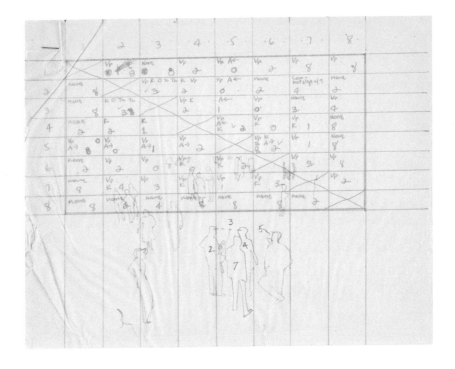

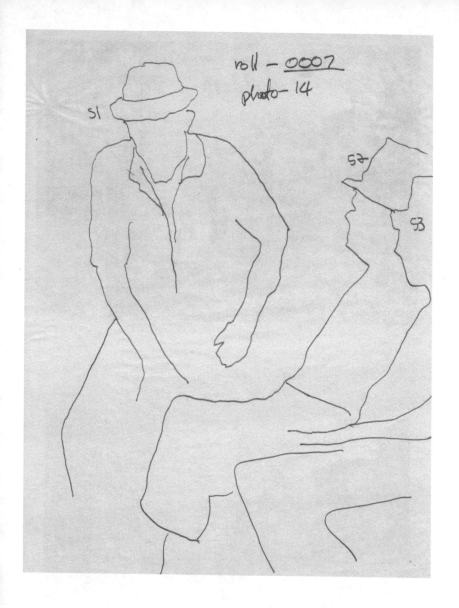

roll – 0007
photo – 14

51

52

53

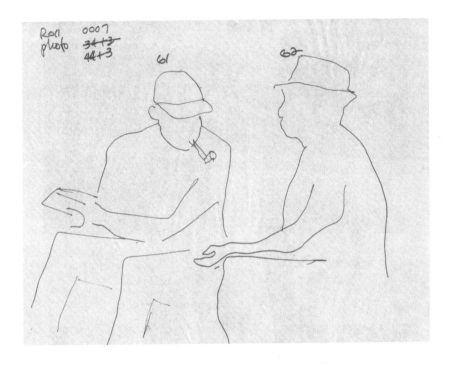

These photos and tracings were taken at an academic conference Hall attended. The event provided many opportunities to observe interactions within the social and public ranges of distance. It is unclear from the comparisons exactly what the value of the tracings was for Hall. What did they potentially allow him to observe that the photos did not? Were they additions to the original images or subtractions?

Roll 1
frame 28

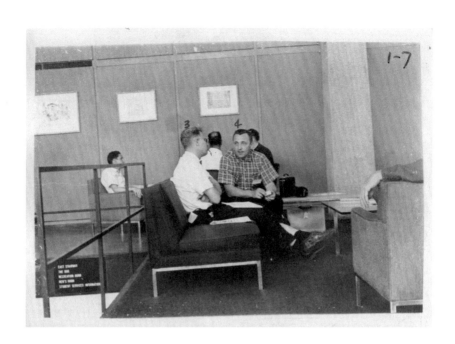

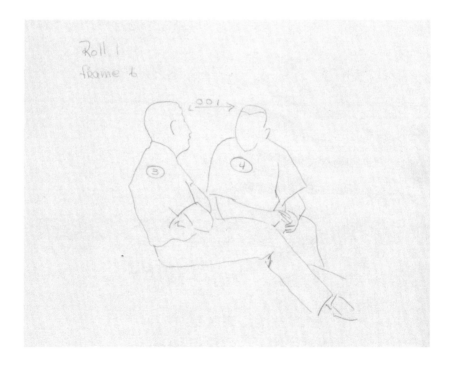

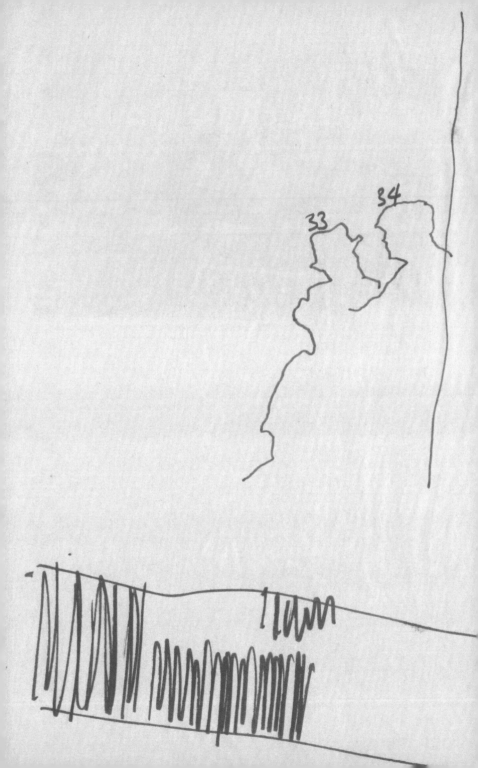

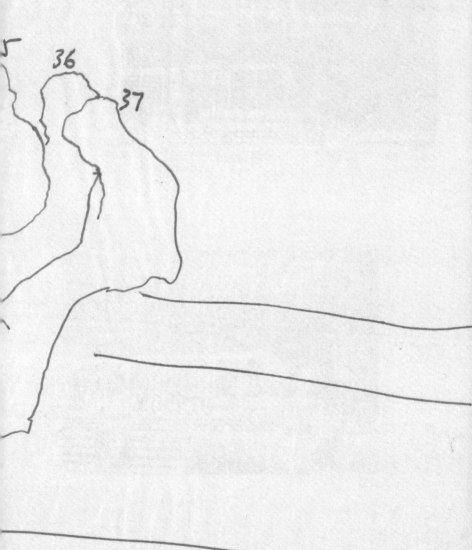

A short sequence taken at Hermann Hall on the IIT campus. Mies van der Rohe's buildings provide a gridded frame and backdrop for these scenes of interaction.

Hall arrived in Chicago as work on Bertrand Goldberg's Marina City was being completed in 1963–64. The two were neighbors and became close friends, developing a lively dialog about the social role of architecture.

From Hall's notes: "White UMC [upper middle class] Chicago (North Side), social occasion, mixed friends & acquaintances. Alcohol may shorten distances somewhat. August 1965 5:30–6:30 pm. Photo Hall Minox."

Buildings and people interact at vastly different scales in this series. In this set, Hall zooms in on Harbour Square, a racially integrated apartment complex in southwest Washington, DC, developed by his client Chloethiel Woodard Smith.

Series 9
Photos and diagrams analyzing the Chicago subway system. Hall
produced these to gather human factors data for Christopher
Alexander's research on San Francisco's BART system.

269

People start forming knots while waiting: inbetween columns, generally out of the way of the flows. Only if they know each other and want to walk, they move toward the middle. After a while, especially during the rush hours between 4.30 pm and 5.30 pm the space right in front of the benches start to fill out first.

Since people once they chose a spot rarely move to make way for incoming flows, and those that are running for trains do not follow the right side but run through free spaces, collisions begin to occur.

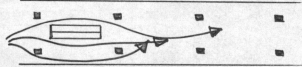

Other cases of collisions occur between people using the transfer machines and those that come running down the stairs to catch the train.
　　　　　　　　　　　　　4.35 - 5.05 pm , Wednesday, March 4
　　　　　　　　　　　　　4.30 - 5.00 pm , Saturday , Feb. 22

During rush hours in the afternoon, when the trains come every three minutes (and passengers of north- and southbound trains run at the same time) collisions increase where the crowds are concentrated.
　　　　　　　　　　　　　4.35 - 5.05 pm , March 3 , Tuesday

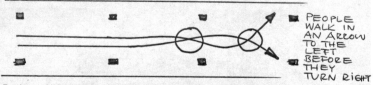

PEOPLE WALK IN AN ARROW TO THE LEFT BEFORE THEY TURN RIGHT

Devices directing and controlling the flows and a better spacial arrangement for waiting regulations can help pull out knots of people from the flows.

On Monroe & State station the space is used both for traffic in both directions and for waiting, since the space inbetween columns fills out quickly. A better arrangement is possible by seperating the traffic and waiting spaces visually. Columns can be such a space — divider.

Movements of passengers on the platform sketch discernible patterns. Perhaps these flows could be redirected toward more pleasant environmental modes of interaction among people and architectural features?

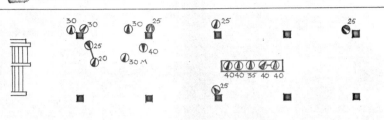

SCALE: 1/8

NUMBER:
ESTIMATED AGE

⊖ MALE WHITE

● MALE NEGRO

⊖ FEMALE WHITE

● FEMALE NEGRO

CONNECTING LINE: CONVERSATION

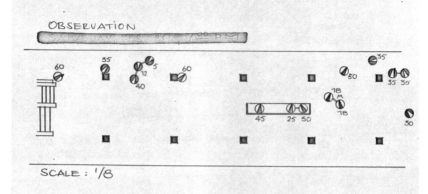

OBSERVATION

SCALE : 1/8

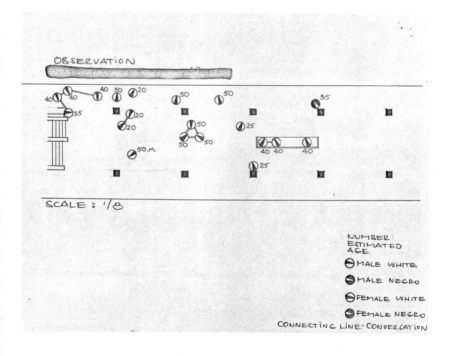

OBSERVATION

SCALE : 1/8

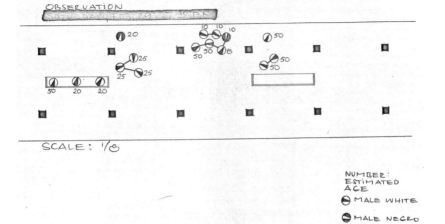

OBSERVATION
SATURDAY, FEB. 29 - 7:40 P.M.

SCALE: 1/8

NUMBER:
ESTIMATED
AGE

⊖ MALE WHITE

⊜ MALE NEGRO

⊖ FEMALE WHITE

⊜ FEMALE NEGRO

CONNECTING LINE: CONVERSATION

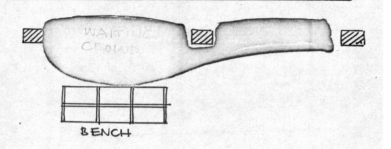

BENCH

Saturday, Feb. 29   7 pm - 7.40 pm

cars: almost all seats taken (Southbound)
      train coming all 6 minutes

alighting: if the platform is not crowded, people rush right into
           the middle of the platform and cause congestions with
           passengers coming out of the adjacent door.

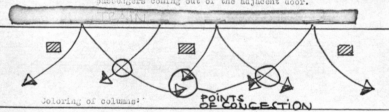

POINTS OF CONGESTION

Coloring of columns:

CTA uses 4 different colors on stations   a cold blue
                                               a deep red
                                               a warm green
                                               a dark brown.

All of these colors destroy the feeling of spaciousness on the station.
These colors emphasize the massiveness of the columns, make them
heavier. The platform appears smaller. Brown and red make the platform extremely uncomfortable. Blue gives it cleanliness and freshness,
but is still to loud.

(C.) ALTERNATE SYSTEM

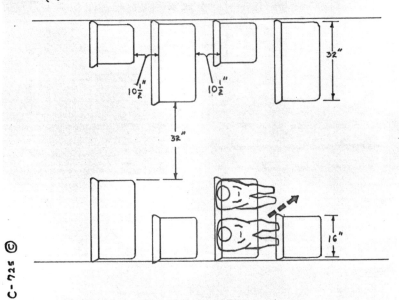

(B.) ARRANGEMENT NEEDED TO USE SEATS EASILY

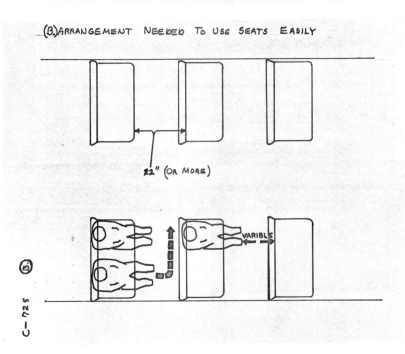

279

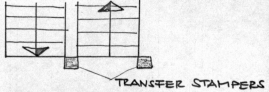

TRANSFER STAMPERS

For boarding and alighting the best, but probably most expensive
solution would be a seperation of the car's doors into boarding
and alighting doors(boarding on one side if the car and alighting
on the other). This might be an expensive solution because for
a two-way station it would require at least three platforms:
1 broad middle platform for boarding in both directions and 2
seperate outer platforms for alighting.

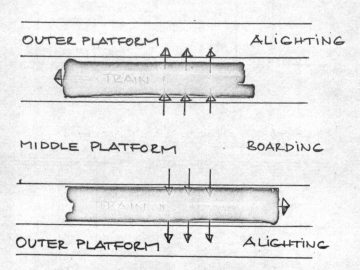

OUTER PLATFORM — ALIGHTING

MIDDLE PLATFORM — BOARDING

OUTER PLATFORM — ALIGHTING

Observation at ticket counter:
Arrangement disadvantageous
The sketch shows the major faults

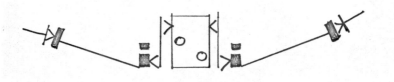

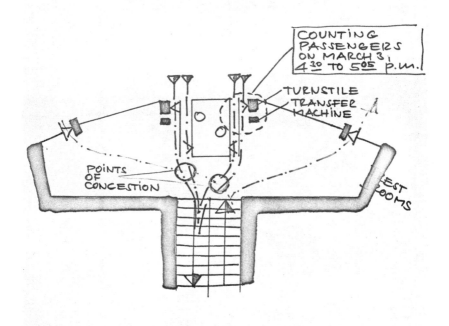

COUNTING
PASSENGERS
ON MARCH 3,
4 30 TO 5 05 p.m.

TURNSTILE
TRANSFER
MACHINE

POINTS
OF
CONCESSION

REST
ROOMS

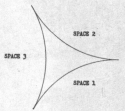

SPACE 2

SPACE 3

SPACE 1

POSSIBLE COLUMN DESIGN FOR LEANING

The footprint of a proposed column design to accommodate the proxemic bubbles of three individuals simultaneously, holding them together in a limited area yet keeping them perceptually insulated.

C-180

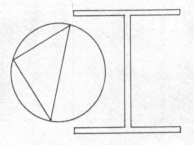

COLUMN OFFERS SECURITY FROM AREAS OUTSIDE
180 VISUAL RANGE

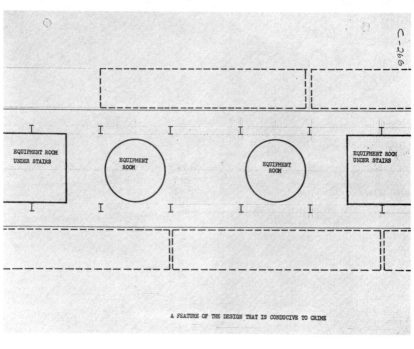

A FEATURE OF THE DESIGN THAT IS CONDUCIVE TO CRIME

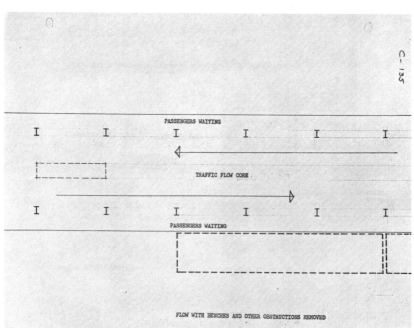

PASSENGERS WAITING

TRAFFIC FLOW CORE

PASSENGERS WAITING

FLOW WITH BENCHES AND OTHER OBSTRUCTIONS REMOVED

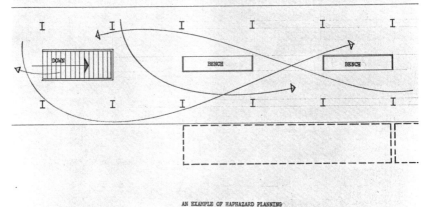

AN EXAMPLE OF HAPHAZARD PLANNING

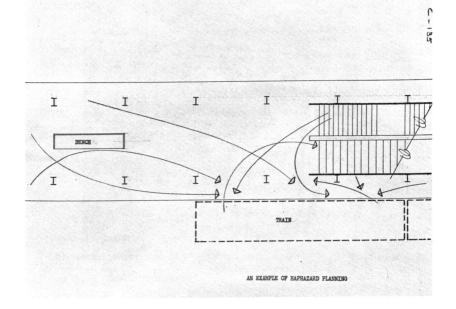

AN EXAMPLE OF HAPHAZARD PLANNING

Series 10
Images Hall collected relating to research facilities at IBM's
Poughkeepsie campus.

IBM gave these photos to Hall to show the strangely proportioned spaces and suboptimal lighting of Building 701.

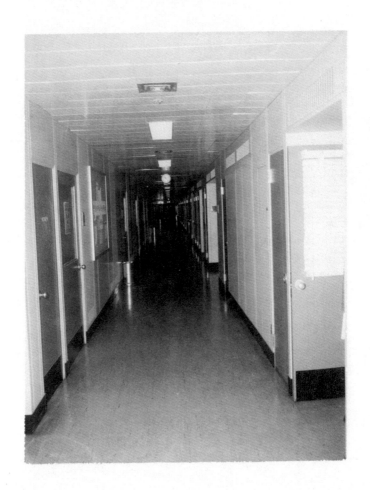

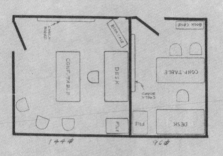

144#   96#

Bldg 702 & 703

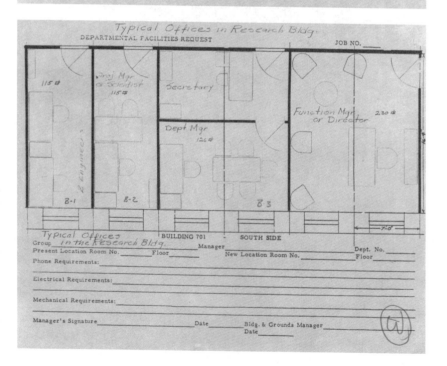

Typical Offices in Research Bldg.

DEPARTMENTAL FACILITIES REQUEST   JOB NO. _____

115 #   Proj Mgr   Secretary   Function Mgr   230 #
          or Scientist   or Director
          115 #

          Engineer's   Dept Mgr
                             126 #

B-1   B-2   B.3   7-0"

Typical Offices   BUILDING 701 -   SOUTH SIDE
Group _in the Research Bldg._   Manager_____
Present Location Room No._____ Floor_____   New Location Room No._____   Dept. No._____
Phone Requirements:_____   Floor_____

Electrical Requirements:_____

Mechanical Requirements:_____

Manager's Signature_____ Date_____ Bldg. & Grounds Manager_____
                                                  Date_____

292

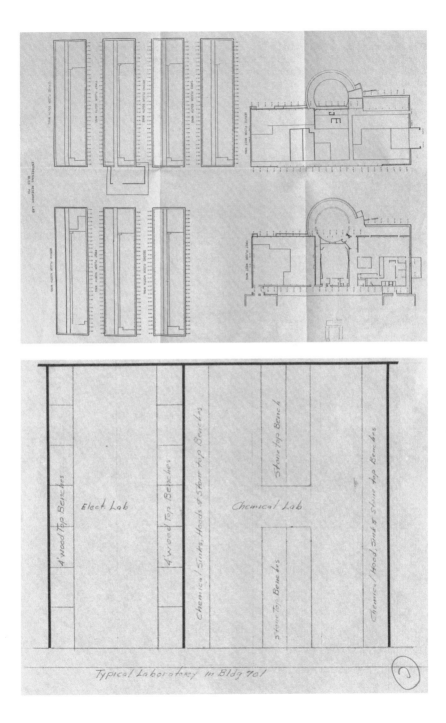

Typical Laboratory in Bldg 701

Series 11
Documentation of a visit to the joint MIT and Harvard Center for Urban Studies around 1963. While there, Hall apparently took photos of the furniture arrangements and did a proxemic study with one of the assistants.

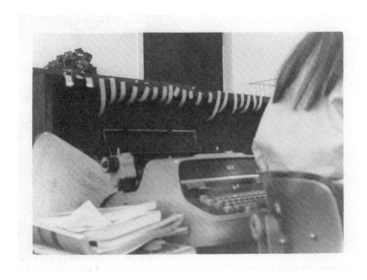

Even though Hall visited the center to speak with its researchers—Kevin Lynch presumably among them—he took the opportunity to photograph offices and workers. At times, the unidentified individuals blend with the furniture.

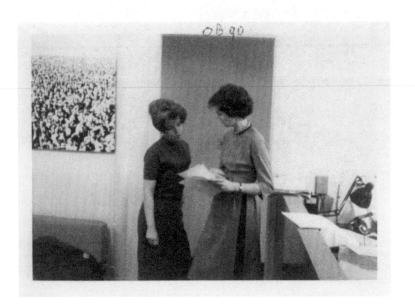

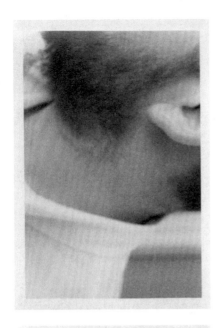 

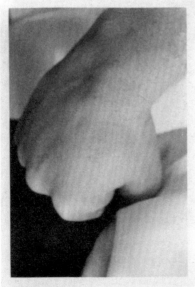 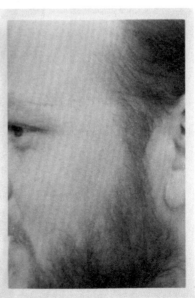

Series 12
Items from uncataloged boxes containing hundreds of images and
documents. The (mostly) interior views feature some well-known
buildings and meditations on architectural space.

N

it is easy to identify who is with whom.

A mysterious set of photos of an empty classroom. Perhaps the desks indicate proxemic forces pulling students toward or away from one another.

Undated photo from the Johnson Wax Building in Racine, Wisconsin.

Proxemic forces at work down the spiral of the Guggenheim Museum.

A batch of images labeled "English model housing." These may have been taken when the Halls visited Ernö Goldfinger and others in England in 1960 or 1961.

327

This set of four medium-format Kodak transparencies of interiors offers no identifying information.

Acknowledgments

I would like to thank James Graham at Columbia Books on Architecture and the City for his faith in this unusual project, and his generous yet critical reading of the text. As the book developed, Joanna Joseph joined the press, and her sympathetic interventions made the process feel truly collaborative. Neil Donnelly and Siiri Tännler's design for the book brought the text and images together in a way that convinced me of the validity of the undertaking. Glenn Perkins edited the manuscript, and I owe him thanks for unmixing my tangled metaphors.

As this is effectively a portrait of a single archive, those people involved in facilitating my access to its materials were of key significance, most especially Roger Myers and Erika Castaño at the University of Arizona Special Collections. Karin Bergh Hall granted permission for me to reproduce the images here. A University of Arizona Provost's award covered costs for scanning images.

Edward Hall's pattern thinking also formed the basis of one chapter in my recent book *The Responsive Environment: Design, Aesthetics, and the Human in the 1970s* (University of Minnesota Press, 2020). Several passages from that text reappear here, and I thank Pieter Martin and Jeff Moen at the press for their encouragement in this regard.

I thank my friends Kate Albers, Dave Sbarra, and Sierra Wong for their encouragement as I ventured into unfamiliar disciplinary territory. And, as ever, I affectionately acknowledge Michelle Strier, and Kase and Ramona Strier Busbea.

Columbia Books on Architecture and the City
An imprint of the Graduate School of
Architecture, Planning, and Preservation

Columbia University
1172 Amsterdam Ave
407 Avery Hall
New York, NY 10027
arch.columbia.edu/books

Distributed by Columbia University Press
cup.columbia.edu

Proxemics and the Architecture of Social Interaction
By Larry D. Busbea

ISBN: 978-1-941332-67-2
Library of Congress Control Number: 2020917915

Graphic Design: Neil Donnelly, Siiri Tännler
Project Editors: James Graham, Joanna Joseph
Image Editor: Emma Macdonald
Copyeditor: Glenn Perkins
Printer: Musumeci, Italy

Director of Publications: Isabelle Kirkham-Lewitt
Associate Editor: Joanna Joseph

This book has been produced through the Office of the Dean,
Amale Andraos, and the Office of Publications at Columbia
University GSAPP.